Glencoe

Literature

Common Core State Standards Edition

Project Practice Book

Glencoe Literature extension projects for

- Common Core State Standards
- College and Career Readiness
- 21st Century Skills

COURSE 4

McGraw Hill Education

Bothell, WA • Chicago, IL • Columbus, OH • New York, NY

glencoe.com

 **Education**

Send all inquiries to:
McGraw-Hill Education
8787 Orion Place
Columbus, OH 43240

ISBN: 978-0-07-661412-7
MHID: 0-07-661412-3

Printed in the United States of America.

3 4 5 6 7 8 9 REL 15 14 13 12 11

Contents

Reading Lessons: Literature

Reading Lessons: Informational Text

Writing Workshops

Vocabulary

Grades 9–10 Common Core State Standards

Reading Lessons: Literature

Group Discussion

The Most Dangerous Game

Richard Connell

Glencoe Literature, pages 20–42

| RL.9–10.10 | Before starting the lesson, read the following selection and complete the lesson activities in *Glencoe Literature.* |

"The Most Dangerous Game" (pages 20–42)

In this lesson you will analyze and discuss the short story "The Most Dangerous Game" by Richard Connell. You will then plan and create a film version of a scene from the story. Through your participation in the discussion and your work on the project, you will practice the following standards:

| RL.9–10.2 | **Key Ideas and Details** |

- Determine a theme or central idea of a text and analyze its development.
- Provide an objective summary of the text.

| RL.9–10.5 | **Craft and Structure** |

- Analyze how the structure of a text and the order of events within it create mystery, tension, or surprise.

Group Discussion

Discussing a short story, such as "The Most Dangerous Game," within a small group can help you grow as a reader and as a member of a learning community. Together, you and other group members can arrive at a better understanding of a selection, its ideas and craft, and its connection to other works and areas of study.

PLAN

| RL.9–10.1.1
W.9–10.9
W9–10.9a
W.9–10.10
L.9–10.1
L.9–10.2
L.9–10.2c | To prepare for discussion, build your content knowledge by examining the selection in greater detail. On your own, write your answers to the questions that follow, as well as any additional questions you think need to be addressed. Your teacher may review your answers before the discussion, so be sure to use complete sentences and correct spelling, punctuation, and capitalization. |

RL.9–10.5 **Plot Structure** As you probably remember, **plot** refers to the sequence of events and actions in a literary work. Many short stories feature **linear,** or time-ordered, plots that follow five stages of development: exposition, rising action, climax, falling action, and resolution.

1. Review the plot diagram and summary you created in *Glencoe Literature,* pages 40–42. To what degree does the plot structure of "The Most Dangerous Game" match the five plot stages of a linear story? Consider if there are any missing stages, shortened stages, or extended stages.

_____

_____

_____

_____

RL.9–10.5 **Flash-Forward** A **flash-forward** is a conversation, an episode, or an event that takes place in the future. A flash-forward interrupts the linear order of events of a story and skips ahead.

2. Identify the flash-forward within "The Most Dangerous Game." What effect did this use of flash-forward have on you as a reader? Explain your thoughts.

_____

_____

_____

_____

RL.9–10.5 **Foreshadowing and Suspense** Authors of spine-tingling tales like "The Most Dangerous Game" often rely on foreshadowing to grab a reader's attention. **Foreshadowing** is an author's use of hints or clues to prepare the reader for events and situations that will happen later in a story. This writing technique helps to generate **suspense,** or a feeling of mystery, tension, or surprise in the reader.

3. How does Richard Connell use foreshadowing throughout the story to suggest that Rainsford is in danger? Complete the chart below. An example has been completed for you.

Setting	Story Passage	Foreshadowed Event or Situation	Effect on Reader
Yacht	"'The old charts call it 'Ship-Trap Island',' Whitney replied. "A suggestive name, isn't it? Sailors have a curious dread of the place.'" (p. 22)	This passage hints at Rainsford's accidental fall overboard and his arrival on the island.	The reader is filled with tension about the mysterious island.
Caribbean Sea			
General Zaroff's Home			
Ship-Trap Island			

4. Does Richard Connell use hints and clues effectively in the story, or does he give too much information away, diminishing your enjoyment? Support your opinion with story details.

_____

_____

_____

_____

_____

RL.9–10.2 **Theme** In literature, **theme** refers to the main message of a work, often expressed as a general statement about life. Some works have a **stated theme,** which is expressed directly. More frequently, works have an **implied theme,** which is revealed gradually through elements such as plot, character, setting, or a combination of these elements.

5. Identify the main theme of "The Most Dangerous Game." Is the theme stated or implied? Support your answer with details from the story.

_____

_____

_____

_____

_____

_____

_____

_____

_____

ASSIGN

RL.9–10.2
RL.9–10.5
SL.9–10.1
SL.9–10.1a
SL.9–10.1c

Meet with your literature group to plan your discussion. Each group member should become the expert on one or more of the questions answered on the previous pages. Each expert will then guide the discussion on his or her question(s). List each group member and the question(s) he or she will become an expert on in the chart below.

Group Member	Question(s) to Present

SL.9–10.1
SL.9–10.1a
SL.9–10.1c

To become an expert on your question(s), spend some extra time thinking about your question(s) and consulting the text for relevant details. Building on your question(s), write down one or two discussion points or related questions for group members to consider as they explore text issues.

_____
_____
_____
_____
_____

Group Discussion

DISCUSS

SL.9–10.1
SL.9–10.1a
SL.9–10.1b
SL.9–10.1c
SL.9–10.1d

Break into your assigned literature group to conduct your discussion. The expert for question 1 should begin by reading aloud the question and leading the discussion in response. Follow this process for each question until you have covered them all.

Remember that literature groups contain room for disagreement. Healthy debate can help all members push their understanding to a new level. Use your time wisely so that you are able to discuss all the questions sufficiently.

In your discussion, follow the guidelines below.

Discussion Guidelines
• Come to discussions prepared; be sure you have carefully and thoroughly answered all questions.
• Express your ideas clearly. When presenting on your question and commenting on others, support your ideas with concrete evidence from the text. Give specific page numbers.
• Work with your group to set rules for discussion and decision making (*e.g.,* informal consensus, taking votes on key issues, presenting alternative views).
• Work with your group to set clear goals and deadlines.
• Create individual roles as needed (*e.g.,* note taker, moderator, etc.).
• Propel conversations by posing and responding to questions that relate the current discussion to broader themes or larger ideas (*e.g.,* fantasy versus reality).
• Actively incorporate others into the discussion; clarify, verify, or challenge ideas and conclusions.
• Respond thoughtfully to diverse perspectives and summarize points of agreement and disagreement.
• Qualify or justify your views and understanding and make new connections in light of the evidence and reasoning presented.

At the end of your discussion, be prepared to share the insights you have gained with your class. On the lines below, briefly summarize the most interesting ideas or insights you heard or experienced during the discussion.

_____

_____

_____

_____

_____

_____

The Most Dangerous Game
Richard Connell

21st Century Skills Project   Movie

Now that you have analyzed and discussed the short story in detail, you will have the opportunity to extend your thinking about it creatively by participating in a group project. Your assignment is to prepare a movie based on a scene from "The Most Dangerous Game." In carrying out this project, you will follow the steps below:

- Choose a scene from the story.
- Create a storyboard to show what information you want to include, how you will present it visually, and how you will handle other aspects of the movie such as voiceover narration and music.
- If resources allow, shoot your movie and present it to your classmates and teacher.

PART 1 Plan a Film Adaptation

Choose a Scene With your group, discuss which scene from "The Most Dangerous Game" you would like to use as the basis for your movie. The scene you choose should clearly demonstrate both foreshadowing and suspense. It should also be long enough to have a running length of two minutes or more when filmed.

On the lines below, summarize the scene that you've chosen. Make sure to include all key information in your work. Also, give page references from the anthology for the scene.

_____

_____

_____

_____

_____

_____

_____

_____

Create a Storyboard A filmmaker uses a storyboard to plan each shot in a movie. Each individual camera shot is sketched out in small boxes to represent the sequence of shots in a scene. This allows everyone to know what the director wants each scene and shot to look like.

21st Century Skills Project

With a small group, create a storyboard for a movie based on a scene from "The Most Dangerous Game." With your group, discuss what characters, dialogue, and scenery you would include in such a movie. Also discuss what kinds of camera shots you would use. Keep in mind that "The Most Dangerous Game" is set chiefly on a small island in the Caribbean Sea during the early 20th century. You may wish to conduct research in books or on the Internet before making decisions about the appearance of Ship-Trap Island, General Zaroff's mansion, and the characters' clothing.

After you've discussed ideas for the movie, create a storyboard showing each shot in the film. Use information from your notes and graphic organizers to help you. You'll need to provide a sketch of how you want each shot to look, as well as notes on any music or sound effects you want included. You will also need to create dialogue notes for some storyboard frames.

- For type of shot, you may want to indicate "wide-angle shot," "high-angle shot," "reaction shot," or "close-up shot."
- For sounds, you may want to indicate snippets of music or sound effects such as the barking of General Zaroff's dogs.

To build each frame within the storyboard, follow a model like the one below.

Type of shot:
_____

Sketch of Shot

Sound:
_____

Dialogue:
_____

Answer the following questions to help guide you.

1. How should we compose each shot of the scene? What do we want the audience to see?

_____

_____

_____

_____

_____

_____

_____

2. What camera angles would best convey the scene? Do we need close-up shots?

_____

_____

_____

_____

_____

_____

_____

3. How will the shots flow together in sequence? Do we want the scene to be jarring to the audience? Do we want the sequence of shots to be smooth?

_____

_____

_____

_____

_____

_____

_____

_____

21st Century Skills Project

4. How will these shots be edited together to create the scene?

_____

_____

_____

_____

_____

_____

_____

_____

5. What kind of sound do we want in the scene? Voiceover narration? Dramatic music? Sound effects?

_____

_____

_____

_____

_____

_____

_____

_____

Present Your Storyboard If you are not going on to Part 2 of this 21st Century Skills project, your teacher may ask you to present your storyboard as the concluding activity of the project. You may also be evaluated on the presentation.

In presenting your storyboard you should provide a running commentary that explains each frame and makes a smooth transition between frames. You may wish to draw on the summary you wrote to help you. To enhance the impact of your presentation, you can also show actual images along with individual frames, or play sound recordings.

Once you have presented your storyboard, your teacher may ask you to turn it in, along with any images, scripts, or recordings you have assembled.

21st Century Skills Project

PART 2 Create a Film Adaptation

RL.9–10.5
SL.9–10.5
After your group has finished Part 1 of this project, use your storyboard to create a movie version of the scene you've chosen from "The Most Dangerous Game." With your group, answer the questions below to help plan the filming of your scene.

1. What location(s) will we use in our movie? Why?

_____

_____

_____

_____

2. Who will play each part in the movie? How will you make casting decisions?

_____

_____

_____

_____

_____

_____

3. What scenery, props, and costumes will we need?

_____

_____

_____

_____

_____

_____

21st Century Skills Project

4. What type of music and sound effects will we use to foreshadow story events or create suspense?

_____

_____

_____

_____

5. What camera angles, lighting, and filming techniques will we use to foreshadow story events or create suspense?

_____

_____

_____

_____

6. What type of video editing software will we use?

_____

_____

_____

_____

7. List the members of your group and the task each person will complete. Some tasks will need the help of more than one person.

Name   **Task**

_____

_____

_____

_____

Present Your Movie After you've filmed and edited your movie, review it for its content, creativity, group work, and communication of ideas. If you have time, make changes to your film to strengthen any areas that seem weak. Then present it to the class.

After you've shown your movie to your class, answer the following questions with your group:

1. What worked well in our movie? Why?

_____

_____

_____

_____

2. What would we change in the planning, creation, and presentation of this movie if we were to do this project again?

_____

_____

_____

_____

_____

Observe and Evaluate As you view your classmates' movies, take notes about the content and effectiveness of their work. Then use your notes to participate in a class discussion.

1. What images and details are most effective? Why?

_____

_____

_____

_____

21st Century Skills Project

2. Are music and sound effects used effectively to foreshadow story events or create suspense? Explain your thoughts.

_____

_____

_____

_____

_____

_____

3. Are camera angles and filming techniques used effectively to foreshadow story events or create suspense? Explain your thoughts.

_____

_____

_____

_____

_____

_____

4. What would you add to or change in the movie? Why?

_____

_____

_____

_____

_____

American History
Judith Ortiz Cofer
Glencoe Literature, pages 208–219

RL.9–10.10 | Before starting the lesson, read the following selection and complete the lesson activities in *Glencoe Literature*.

"American History" (pages 208–219)

In this lesson you will analyze and discuss Judith Ortiz Cofer's short story "American History." You will then create a slide show that reflects an aspect of the story. Through your participation in the discussion and your work on the project, you will practice the following standards:

RL9–10.2
RL.9–10.3 | **Key Ideas and Details**
- Determine a theme or central idea of a text and analyze its development.
- Provide an objective summary of the text.
- Analyze how complex characters develop, interact with other characters, and advance the plot or develop the theme.

Group Discussion

Discussing a short story, such as "American History," within a small group can help you grow as a reader and as a member of a learning community. Together, you and other group members can arrive at a better understanding of a selection, its ideas and craft, and its connection to other works and areas of study.

PLAN

RL.9–10.1
W.9–10.9
W.9–10.9a
W.9–10.10
L.9–10.1
L.9–10.2
L.9–10.2c | To prepare for discussion, build your content knowledge by examining the selection in greater detail. On your own, write your answers to the questions that follow using text evidence. You may also write additional questions about the selection that you wish to discuss with your group. Your teacher may review your answers before the discussion, so be sure to use correct grammar, spelling, punctuation, and capitalization.

RL.9–10.3 | **Character** A **character** is an individual in a work of fiction. One way of learning about a character is to consider his or her **motivation**—the reason a character thinks, acts, or feels a certain way. Sometimes a character's motivation is stated directly in a story. More often, though, a character's motivation is implied and the reader needs to use clues within the story to figure it out. During the course of a story, a character may develop multiple motivations; sometimes these motivations conflict with one another.

1. In the chart below, identify the actions of the story's characters following the death of President Kennedy. Then, explain the characters' motivations for their actions. Include the clues from the story that helped you determine the characters' motivations. An example has been completed for you.

Character	Action(s) Following the President's Death	Motivation for Action(s)	Clues from the Story that Suggest Motivation
Big girl	She yells and picks up her books.	She isn't concerned about the president's death. Instead, she's happy to be let out of school early.	She cries out, which shows her excitement.
Mr. De Palma			
Elena's mother			
Elena			
Eugene's mother			

2. Using your completed chart, compare and contrast Elena's response to the tragedy with the responses of the other characters. Is Elena's response similar to or different from the responses of other characters? Explain your thoughts.

_____

_____

_____

_____

3. Do you think Elena's response following the tragedy seems reasonable? Why or why not?

_____

_____

_____

_____

_____

4. Why does Elena feel conflicted, or confused, in her motivation? Explain your thoughts.

_____

_____

_____

_____

5. In what ways has Elena's motivation for watching the house next door to El Building changed during the course of the story? Explain your thoughts.

_____

_____

_____

_____

_____

Group Discussion

RL.9–10.2
RL.9–10.3

Theme A story's **theme** is its message about life, the world, or human nature. An author may not state the theme directly. Instead, the author may imply the theme through details of setting, character, and plot. A story may have more than one theme.

6. A story's theme(s) can often become clearer if you summarize the work first. Use the lines below to summarize "American History." Remember that a summary only includes the main events and explains the main characters' problems and how they are resolved. Do not include personal opinions or comments.

_____

_____

_____

_____

_____

_____

_____

_____

_____

7. What is the main theme of "American History"? How does Ortiz Cofer develop this theme through the story's characters and title? Support your answer with details from the story.

_____

_____

_____

_____

_____

_____

_____

_____

_____

ASSIGN

Meet with your literature group to plan your discussion. Each group member should become the expert on one or more of the questions answered on the previous pages. Each expert will then guide the discussion on his or her question(s). List each group member and the question(s) he or she will become an expert on in the following chart.

Group Member	Question(s) to Present

To become an expert on your question(s), spend some extra time thinking about your question(s) and consulting the text for relevant details. Building on your question(s), write down one or two discussion points or related questions for group members to consider as they explore text issues.

_____

_____

_____

_____

_____

_____

DISCUSS

SL.9–10.1
SL.9–10.1a
SL.9–10.1b
SL.9–10.1c
SL.9–10.1d

Break into your assigned literature group to conduct your discussion. The expert for question 1 should begin by reading aloud the question and leading the discussion in response. Follow this process for each question until you have covered them all.

Remember that literature groups contain room for disagreement. Healthy debate can help all members push their understanding to a new level. Use your time wisely so that you are able to discuss all the questions sufficiently.

In your discussion, follow the guidelines below.

Discussion Guidelines

- Come to discussions prepared; be sure you have carefully and thoroughly answered all questions.

- Express your ideas clearly. When presenting on your question and commenting on others, support your ideas with concrete evidence from the text. Give specific page numbers.

- Work with your group to set rules for discussion and decision making (*e.g.,* informal consensus, taking votes on key issues, presenting alternative views).

- Work with your group to set clear goals and deadlines.

- Create individual roles as needed (*e.g.,* note taker, moderator, etc.).

- Propel conversations by posing and responding to questions that relate the current discussion to broader themes or larger ideas (*e.g.,* fantasy versus reality).

- Actively incorporate others into the discussion; clarify, verify, or challenge ideas and conclusions.

- Respond thoughtfully to diverse perspectives and summarize points of agreement and disagreement.

- Qualify or justify your views and understanding and make new connections in light of the evidence and reasoning presented.

At the end of your discussion, be prepared to share the insights you have gained with your class. On the lines below, briefly summarize the most interesting ideas or insights you heard or experienced during the discussion.

_____

_____

_____

_____

_____

American History
Judith Ortiz Cofer

21st Century Skills Project   Slide Show

Now that you have analyzed and discussed "American History" in detail, you will have the opportunity to extend your thinking about it creatively by completing a group project.

Your assignment is to tell Elena's story through a collection of images and accompanying commentary. In carrying out this project, you will follow the steps below:

- Find and select images that convey Elena's experiences as described in the story. You may use fine art or photographic representations.
- Plan and write commentary that explains the images you've chosen and their connection to Elena.
- Present your work in a slide show, if resources allow.

PART 1 Image Search

With a small group, find images that correspond to the key people, places, and events within Elena's life. Then write a presentation in which you explain how the images show Elena's development from a romantic girl to a more worldly-wise young adult.

RL.9–10.3
W.9–10.6

Find and Select Images Conduct a search online or in print books to find images that effectively convey Elena's experiences and her growth over the course of the story. You might wish to conduct a broad search first to see what types of images are available. Then narrow your findings to match particular details from the story. Keep in mind that you should gather a variety of images, including fine art (paintings, sculptures, artifacts, etc.) and photographs (historical images, advertising images, etc.). Here are aspects of Elena's life from "American History" you might wish to focus on:

- El Building/1960's Puerto Rican culture
- Eugene/first love
- Eugene's house
- Elena's mother
- President Kennedy's death/1960's American culture
- Eugene's mother

After you've gathered a reasonable number of images (10 to 12 images), go through them with your group and pick the most suitable examples. You'll want to have 6 to 8 images in total. Use the following image chart to record your final choices.

Aspect of Elena's Life	Corresponding Image	Type of Image	Reason for Choosing Image

RL.9–10.3 | **Organize Images and Plan Commentary** Once you've selected your images with your group, you'll need to consider how you'd like to arrange them to best tell Elena's story. Remember that you'll want to convey Elena's growth over the course of the story. Do you want to show each image by itself, or do you want to group some images together? After you've decided on your image organization, plan your corresponding commentary. Keep in mind that your images and commentary are meant to work together to create an effective presentation.

Write Commentary Decide which group members will be responsible for writing each part of the commentary. Use your image chart to guide you as you write. Remember not to overload each slide with too much text. Include a title for your presentation and use bulleted lists and headings to make your commentary reader-friendly.

After all the content is written, peer review each other's work and make sure it all flows together well and shows clear connections between the images and the story. Remember to credit your image sources.

Present Your Commentary If you are not going on to Part 2 of the 21st Century Skills Project, your teacher may ask you to present your images and commentary as the end result of the project. You may also be evaluated on the presentation.

Present your commentary in a written or typed format that is visually appealing and offers the information clearly. Include print-outs of the necessary images and include them at point of use with your commentary. Once your group is satisfied that the content is presented effectively, turn it in to your teacher.

21st Century Skills Project

PART 2 Create a Slide Show

RL. 9–10.3
SL.9–10.5

After you've finished Part 1 of this project, create your brief slide show (3 to 4 minutes in length) based on your image chart and commentary.

Make sure the information in your slide show is visually appealing, clearly presented, and flows together logically. Also, make sure that images are interwoven with the text in a way that makes sense. Consider adding background music or sound effects to enhance your ideas.

Rehearse your presentation in front of friends or family members before presenting to your class. Make sure that each person in your group knows which portions of the presentation he or she is responsible for. As you rehearse, make sure the transitions between presenters are smooth.

After you've completed this project, answer the following questions.

1. How well does your slide show tell Elena's experiences and her development over the course of the story?

_____

_____

_____

_____

_____

_____

_____

2. Does your slide show flow well? Is information presented clearly? Explain your thoughts.

_____

_____

_____

_____

_____

_____

_____

_____

3. What would you change in the planning, creation, and presentation of this project if you were to do it again?

_____

_____

_____

_____

_____

_____

_____

_____

_____

_____

Evaluate As you read and view your classmates' work, take notes about the content and effectiveness of their slide show presentations. Then use your notes to participate in a class discussion about the project.

1. Does the slide show effectively convey Elena's development from a romantic girl to a more worldly-wise young adult? Why or why not?

_____

_____

_____

_____

_____

_____

_____

_____

21st Century Skills Project

2. Is the information in the slide show presented clearly and effectively? Explain your thoughts.

_____

_____

_____

_____

_____

_____

_____

_____

_____

3. What would you add or change in the slide show? Why? Consider content and organization.

_____

_____

_____

_____

_____

_____

_____

_____

_____

21st Century Skills Project

Sympathy

Paul Laurence Dunbar

Glencoe Literature, pages 531–535

RL.9–10.10 Before starting the lesson, read the following selection and complete the lesson activities in *Glencoe Literature.*

"Sympathy" (pages 531–535)

In this lesson you will analyze and discuss Paul Laurence Dunbar's poem "Sympathy." You will then write a poem of your own that you can publish online. Through your participation in the discussion and your work on the project, you will practice the following standards:

RL.9–10.4 **Craft and Structure**

- Determine the meaning of words and phrases as they are used in the text, including figurative and connotative meanings.
- Analyze the cumulative impact of specific word choices on meaning and tone.

Group Discussion

Discussing a poem, such as "Sympathy," within a small group can help you grow as a reader and as a member of a learning community. Together, you and other group members can arrive at a better understanding of a selection, its ideas and craft, and its connection to other works and areas of study.

PLAN

RL.9–10.1
W.9–10.9
W.9–10.9a
W.9–10.10
L.9–10.1
L.9–10.2
L.9–10.2c

To prepare for discussion, build your content knowledge by examining the selection in greater detail. On your own, write your answers to the questions that follow using text evidence. You may also write additional questions about the selection that you wish to discuss with your group. Your teacher may review your answers before the discussion, so be sure to use correct grammar, spelling, punctuation, and capitalization.

RL.9–10.4 **Diction** An author's **diction,** or word choice, is an important aspect of his or her writing style. Diction can be described as formal or informal, friendly or detached, or a number of other ways. Poets often rely on diction to help them create compact works of great power.

1. How would you describe the diction in "Sympathy"? Support your response with evidence from the text.

   _____

   _____

   _____

RL.9–10.4
L.9–10.5
L.9–10.5b
Denotation and Connotation The **denotation** of a word refers to its literal definition, or its meaning in the dictionary. The **connotation** of a word refers to the attitudes or feelings associated with it. For example, both *brilliance* and *glare* may be defined as "excessively bright," but *glare* has a negative connotation that *brilliance* does not. A word may carry a negative, neutral, or positive connotation. Connotations of words can have an important influence on style and meaning and are particularly important in poetry.

2. Several words from the poem are listed in the chart below. In the appropriate columns, list each word's denotation and its connotation(s) in the context of the poem. Then explain how these connotations affect the overall mood, or feeling of the poem.

Word	Denotation	Connotation
sympathy (title)		
caged (lines 1, 7, 8, 15, 21)		
bright (line 2)		
beats (lines 8, 14)		
Overall Mood		

RL.9–10.4
L.9–10.5
L.9–10.5a

Figurative Language In literature, **figurative language** is language used for descriptive effect, often to imply meaning. Expressions of figurative language are not literally true but express some truth beyond the literal level. All writers use figurative language, although it is particularly important to poets, who rely on it to bring power and vitality to their writing. Types of figurative language include personification, similes, metaphors and extended metaphors.

3. A **metaphor** is a comparison between two unlike things. However, in a metaphor, the comparison is implied rather than stated. There is no use of connective words such as *like* or *as*. Identify the example of metaphor in lines 5–6. What comparison is made? What subject(s) does it help you to see in a new way?

_____

_____

_____

_____

_____

_____

_____

4. An **extended metaphor** is a comparison that is carried out throughout a paragraph, a stanza, or an entire work. Some literary critics believe "Sympathy" is an extended metaphor that compares the experiences of a caged bird to those of African Americans living during the time of slavery and after as free people struggling to fit into society. What details from the poem support this interpretation?

_____

_____

_____

_____

_____

_____

Group Discussion

Imagery is descriptive language that appeals to one or more of the five senses: sight, sound, touch, taste, and smell. Imagery helps create an emotional response in the reader.

5. In the chart below, list examples of imagery from "Sympathy" that appeal to the five senses. Give one example for each sense. Then explain what each example means.

Sense	Example of Imagery	Meaning
Sight		
Hearing		
Touch		
Taste		
Smell		

RL.9–10.4 | **Tone** An author's attitude toward his or her subject is called **tone.** It is conveyed through elements such as diction and figurative language. A writer's tone may be described in a variety of ways, such as sympathetic, serious, ironic, sad, bitter, and so on.

6. How would you describe the tone of "Sympathy"? How do the author's specific word choices throughout the poem contribute to this tone?

_____

_____

_____

_____

_____

_____

ASSIGN

RL.9–10.4
L.9–10.5
L.9–10.5a
L.9–10.5b
SL.9–10.1
SL.9–10.1a
SL.9–10.1c

Meet with your literature group to plan your discussion. Each group member should become the expert on one or more of the questions answered on the previous pages. Each expert will then guide the discussion on his or her question(s). List each group member and the question(s) he or she will become an expert on in the chart below.

Group Member	Question(s) to Present

To become an expert on your question(s), spend some extra time thinking about your question(s) and consulting the text for relevant details. Building on your question(s), write down one or two discussion points or related questions for group members to consider as they explore text issues.

_____

_____

_____

_____

_____

_____

DISCUSS

SL.9–10.1a
SL.9–10.1b
SL.9–10.1c
SL.9–10.1d

Break into your assigned literature group to conduct your discussion. The expert for question 1 should begin by reading aloud the question and leading the discussion in response. Follow this process for each question until you have covered them all.

Remember that literature groups contain room for disagreement. Healthy debate can help all members push their understanding to a new level. Use your time wisely so that you are able to discuss all the questions sufficiently.

In your discussion, follow the guidelines below.

Discussion Guidelines
• Come to discussions prepared; be sure you have carefully and thoroughly answered all questions.
• Express your ideas clearly. When presenting on your question and commenting on others, support your ideas with concrete evidence from the text. Give specific page numbers.
• Work with your group to set rules for discussion and decision making (*e.g.,* informal consensus, taking votes on key issues, presenting alternative views).
• Work with your group to set clear goals and deadlines.
• Create individual roles as needed (*e.g.,* note taker, moderator, etc.).
• Propel conversations by posing and responding to questions that relate the current discussion to broader themes or larger ideas (*e.g.,* fantasy versus reality).
• Actively incorporate others into the discussion; clarify, verify, or challenge ideas and conclusions.
• Respond thoughtfully to diverse perspectives and summarize points of agreement and disagreement.
• Qualify or justify your views and understanding and make new connections in light of the evidence and reasoning presented.

At the end of your discussion, be prepared to share the insights you have gained with your class. On the lines below, briefly summarize the most interesting ideas or insights you heard or experienced during the discussion.

_____

_____

_____

_____

_____

_____

Sympathy
Paul Laurence Dunbar

21st Century Skills Project Multimedia Poem

Now that you have analyzed and discussed the poem in detail, you will have the opportunity to extend your thinking about it creatively by completing a project. Your assignment is to write a poem. If resources allow, you can publish your poem online.

PART 1 Write a Poem

RL.9–10.4 Using "Sympathy" as a model, write a poem that portrays a person, place, or thing in a symbolic way. If necessary, review information on *symbol* within *Glencoe Literature,* pages 532–535. If you publish your poem online later, you'll be able to add links to pictures and other media to help elaborate on the details in your poem.

To help you plan your poem, fill out the graphic organizer on the next page. Consider these questions as you fill it out:

- What person, place, or thing will I write about? What symbolic meaning do I want to convey through it?
- Will I write in a form (such as a sonnet), or will my poem be free verse?
- Will my poem have a **meter** (a regular pattern of stressed and unstressed syllables)?
- Will it have a **rhyme scheme** (the pattern of rhyme formed by the end rhymes)?
- What types of imagery and figurative language will I use?
- What overall tone would I like to convey?

21st Century Skills Project

Person/Place/Thing:	
Symbolic Meaning:	
Speaker:	Form:
Meter:	Line Lengths:
Number of Stanzas:	Rhyme Scheme:
Overall Tone:	

Imagery/Figurative Language	How It Contributes to Tone

Freewrite Before you begin drafting your poem, you might find it helpful to freewrite what you want to say in prose. Focus on getting all your thoughts down without editing yourself. After you've written what you want to say, go back and highlight key images and vivid descriptions that would work well in your poem.

Draft As you write your poem, keep the following tips in mind:

- Begin drafting by writing the first line of your poem. Ideally, your first line should identify the person, place, or thing you're writing about and establish your tone.

- Choose your words carefully. Use vivid, concrete images that appeal to the senses and make sure your images and figurative language communicate your desired tone.

- Convey your ideas as precisely as possible and avoid unnecessary words.

- If you're using stanzas, each one should convey a cohesive idea and these ideas should progress or flow from one stanza to the next. Consider saving your most powerful image for your final stanza or last line.

- Make sure your ending provides a sense of completion to the poem and that it is consistent with the message you've been conveying throughout.

- After you're done, choose a title for your poem.

Present Your Poem If you are not going on to Part 2 of the 21st Century Skills Project, your teacher may ask you to present your poem orally as the end result of the project. You may also be evaluated on the presentation.

Before you present your poem to the class, practice reading it aloud on your own and in front of family members or friends. Don't rush your reading. Use your punctuation and line breaks to help you determine when to pause. Speak clearly and look at your audience. Try to memorize some, if not all, of your poem so that you don't have to read off your paper throughout your presentation. Vary your intonation to get your meaning across and to emphasize certain words or ideas.

21st Century Skills Project

PART 2 Publish Online

SL.9–10.5

After you've finished Part 1 of this project, publish your poem online in an interactive format that includes an audio recording of your poem and hyperlinks to images and other visual media (such as video clips).

SL.9–10.6

Audio Recording Before you record your poem, practice reading it aloud. Don't rush as you read. Use your punctuation and line breaks to determine where to pause. Be sure to adapt your speech to the context. For example, if your poem is written using formal language and standard grammar, don't read it with an informal tone of voice. When you feel prepared, record your poem.

Links to Visual Media When you publish your poem, you will include hyperlinks to visual media, which will elaborate on the images and details you've included in your poem. These links will help your readers get a better understanding of the subject you wrote about. For example, if you wrote a poem about New York City that included imagery of the Statue of Liberty, you might link that image to a photo of the famous landmark.

Before you publish your poem, fill in the chart below to help you decide what links you want to include in your work.

Image/Detail in Poem	Line Number(s)	Corresponding Visual Media Link

21st Century Skills Project

W.9–10.6 **Publish and Present** After you've completed your chart, decide where you will publish your poem. If your school already has a Web site for student work, you might consider publishing your poem there. You can also search online for Web sites that allow you to create your own page for free. These types of sites often provide templates and are easy to use.

Publish your poem on your chosen site. Using your chart as a guide, hyperlink various images in your poem to photos, fine art, and other media. Add a hyperlink to your audio recording at the beginning of the poem. When you're finished, send the URL of your site to your teacher and classmates so they can read and view your work.

After you've completed this project, answer the following questions.

1. Describe the use of symbolism in your poem.

_____

_____

_____

_____

_____

_____

_____

_____

2. How does your audio recording add to the presentation of your poem?

_____

_____

_____

_____

_____

_____

_____

_____

21st Century Skills Project

3. Which images in your poem led to the most interesting links? Why?

_____

_____

_____

_____

_____

_____

_____

_____

4. What would you change in the planning, creation, and presentation of this project if you were to do it again?

_____

_____

_____

_____

_____

_____

_____

_____

_____

_____

_____

21st Century Skills Project

Evaluate Read your classmates' poems once without clicking on any of the links so that you understand the content of the poems. Then read the poems a second time and click on the links to see the media and hear the audio recording. As you read and view your classmates' work, take notes about the content and effectiveness of their poems and visual media. Then use your notes to participate in a class discussion about the project.

1. How well does the poem use symbolism? Is the use of symbolism exciting and innovative? Explain.

_____

_____

_____

_____

_____

_____

_____

_____

_____

2. Does the audio recording add to or detract from your understanding of the poem? Explain.

_____

_____

_____

_____

_____

_____

_____

_____

_____

21st Century Skills Project

3. How well do the links to visual media connect to images/details in the poem? Explain.

_____

_____

_____

_____

_____

_____

_____

_____

_____

_____

_____

4. What would you add or change in the poem or the accompanying visual media? Why?

_____

_____

_____

_____

_____

_____

_____

_____

_____

_____

_____

The Tragedy of Romeo and Juliet

William Shakespeare

Glencoe Literature, pages 624–743

RL.9–10.10 Before starting the lesson, read the following selection and complete the lesson activities in *Glencoe Literature.*

The Tragedy of Romeo and Juliet **(pages 624–743)**

In this lesson you will analyze and discuss William Shakespeare's *Romeo and Juliet.* You will then plan and create a slide show in which you compare and contrast representations of subjects or key scenes from the written play with the equivalent subjects and scenes in art. Through your participation in the discussion and your work on the project, you will practice the following standards:

RL.9–10.3 | **Key Ideas and Details**
- Analyze how complex characters develop, interact with other characters, and advance the plot.

RL.9–10.5 | **Craft and Structure**
- Analyze how the structure of a text and the order of events within it create mystery, tension, or surprise.

RL.9–10.7
RL.9–10.9 | **Integration of Knowledge and Ideas**
- Analyze the representation of subjects or scenes in two different artistic mediums.
- Analyze how an author draws on and transforms source material.

Group Discussion

Discussing a play, such as *Romeo and Juliet*, within a small group can help you grow as a reader and as a member of a learning community. Together, you and other group members can arrive at a better understanding of a selection, its ideas and craft, and its connection to other works and areas of study.

Group Discussion

PLAN

RL.9–10.1
W.9–10.9
W.9–10.9a
W.9–10.10
L.9–10.1
L.9–10.2
L.9–10.2c

To prepare for discussion, build your content knowledge by examining the selection in greater detail. On your own, write your answers to the questions that follow using text evidence. You may also write additional questions about the selection that you wish to discuss with your group. Your teacher may review your answers before the discussion, so be sure to use correct grammar, spelling, punctuation, and capitalization.

RL.9–10.3 **Tragic Hero** In tragedy, the main character, or **tragic hero,** is brought to ruin or suffers a great sorrow as a result of a fatal character flaw, errors in judgment, or forces beyond human control. Traditionally, the tragic hero is a person of high rank, who, out of an exaggerated sense of power and pride, violates a human, natural, or divine law. By breaking the law the hero poses a threat to society and causes the suffering or death of family members, friends, and associates. Shakespeare's *Romeo and Juliet* is an unusual tragedy in that it portrays two tragic heroes: Romeo and Juliet.

1. What qualities define Romeo as a tragic hero? Juliet? Support your responses with evidence from the play.

   Romeo: _____

   _____

   _____

   Juliet: _____

   _____

   _____

2. What is Romeo's tragic flaw? Juliet's? Explain your thoughts.

   Romeo's flaw: _____

   _____

   _____

   Juliet's flaw: _____

   _____

   _____

RL.9–10.3 **Foil** A character who provides a strong contrast to another character is called a **foil.** *Romeo* and *Juliet* contains several pairs of foils.

3. Review Act 1, Scene 4 (pages 644–647). Identify how Mercutio is a foil to Romeo. How does the contrast between the two men reveal Romeo's weaknesses?

_____

_____

_____

_____

_____

_____

4. Identify the values you think Romeo and Mercutio each represent. How do these values relate to one of the main themes, or messages about life, of the play?

_____

_____

_____

_____

_____

_____

5. Identify another pair of foils within *Romeo and Juliet*. Why do you suppose Shakespeare uses numerous pairs of foils within this tragedy? Explain your thoughts.

_____

_____

_____

_____

_____

Group Discussion

RL.9–10.5 | **Juxtaposition** A common technique used within Elizabethan drama, such as Shakespeare's *Romeo and Juliet,* is **juxtaposition** —the placement of two or more distinct elements side by side in order to contrast or compare them. In *Romeo and Juliet,* Shakespeare purposely juxtaposes contrasting scenes in order to create mystery, tension, or surprise.

6. Review Act 2, scenes 1–2 of *Romeo and Juliet* (pages 656–664). Describe the ways these scenes contrast. What effect does this example of juxtaposition create?

_____

_____

_____

_____

_____

RL.9–10.5 | **Pacing** The speed with which the action proceeds in a narrative is called **pacing.** Skilled dramatists carefully pace the events in their plays so that the audience does not learn too much too soon but doesn't become bored either.

7. How does the pacing of *Romeo and Juliet* contribute to a feeling of mystery, tension, or surprise?

_____

_____

_____

_____

RL.9–10.9 | **Source Material** According to literary scholars, Shakespeare drew his material for *Romeo and Juliet* primarily from Arthur Brooke's narrative poem *The Tragicall Historye of Romeus and Juliet,* published in 1562. In fact, Shakespeare's play is very similar to Brooke's poem—adapting the plot, characters, and sometimes even the characters' speeches from the earlier work. In Shakespeare's hands, however, the story became a groundbreaking example of Elizabethan drama. Shakespeare condensed the timeframe of the story, developed the story's title characters and their relationships, magnified other characters, and added new characters—all to great effect.

8. Reread the Build Background information on pages 625 and 655 of your textbook. Then read the chart below to learn details of Brooke's poem. Fill in the chart to show how these details are utilized and transformed in Shakespeare's play. An example has been completed for you.

Brooke's Poem	Shakespeare's Play
The events within Brooke's poem take place over the course of about nine months.	The events of Shakespeare's play take place over the course of about five days (Sunday–Thursday). This information is conveyed through the play's scene openings.
Juliet is 16 years old.	
Juliet's nurse is an intelligent and gracious character within the poem.	
Mercutio is a character who appears only briefly within the poem. He is described as a courtier who is "bold. . .among the bashful maids" at the Capulet Christmas feast (line 258).	
County Paris is a character who appears only briefly within the poem. He and Capulet strike an agreement for Juliet's hand in marriage (lines 1876–1881)	
The characters of Samson, Balthasar, Gregory, and Potpan do not appear within the poem.	

9. What effect does Shakespeare's condensed timeframe create? Explain your thoughts.

_____

_____

_____

_____

Group Discussion

10. What effect does Juliet's youth create? Explain your thoughts.

_____

_____

_____

_____

11. Why do you suppose Shakespeare chose to make the character of Juliet's nurse different from the version within Brooke's poem?

_____

_____

_____

_____

12. Why do you suppose Shakespeare chose to expand existing characters or create new characters?

_____

_____

_____

_____

RL.9–10.7 **Artistic Mediums** Movies, creative writing, fine art, and music are all examples of different **artistic mediums,** or forms of artistic expression. When you compare the representation of a subject or key scene in two different artistic mediums, you can see how each artist chose to interpret the subject or scene as well as what each artist emphasized or left out.

13. Examine the image that shows the activity within the Capulet home following the feigned death of Juliet on page 720 of your textbook. How does this painting compare with the same scene as it is written in the play?

_____

_____

_____

_____

ASSIGN

RL.9–10.3
RL.9–10.5
RL.9–10.7
RL.9–10.9
SL.9–10.1
SL.9–10.1a

Meet with your literature group to plan your discussion. Each group member should become the expert on one or more of the questions answered on the previous pages. Each expert will then guide the discussion on his or her question(s). List each group member and the question(s) he or she will become an expert on in the chart below.

Group Member	Question(s) to Present

To become an expert on your question(s), spend some extra time thinking about your question(s) and consulting the text for relevant details. Building on your question(s), write down one or two discussion points or related questions for group members to consider as they explore text issues.

_____

_____

_____

_____

_____

_____

DISCUSS

SL.9–10.1
SL.9–10.1a
SL.9–10.1b
SL.9–10.1c
SL.9–10.1d

Break into your assigned literature group to conduct your discussion. The expert for question 1 should begin by reading aloud the question and leading the discussion in response. Follow this process for each question until you have covered them all.

Remember that literature groups contain room for disagreement. Healthy debate can help all members push their understanding to a new level. Use your time wisely so that you are able to discuss all the questions sufficiently.

In your discussion, follow the guidelines below.

Discussion Guidelines

- Come to discussions prepared; be sure you have carefully and thoroughly answered all questions.

- Express your ideas clearly. When presenting on your question and commenting on others, support your ideas with concrete evidence from the text. Give specific page numbers.

- Work with your group to set rules for discussion and decision making (*e.g.*, informal consensus, taking votes on key issues, presenting alternative views).

- Work with your group to set clear goals and deadlines.

- Create individual roles as needed (*e.g.*, note taker, moderator, etc.).

- Propel conversations by posing and responding to questions that relate the current discussion to broader themes or larger ideas (*e.g.*, fantasy versus reality).

- Actively incorporate others into the discussion; clarify, verify, or challenge ideas and conclusions.

- Respond thoughtfully to diverse perspectives and summarize points of agreement and disagreement.

- Qualify or justify your views and understanding and make new connections in light of the evidence and reasoning presented.

At the end of your discussion, be prepared to share the insights you have gained with your class. On the lines below, briefly summarize the most interesting ideas or insights you heard or experienced during the discussion.

_____

_____

_____

_____

_____

_____

The Tragedy of Romeo and Juliet
William Shakespeare

21st Century Skills Project Slide Show

Now that you have analyzed and discussed the play in detail, you will have the opportunity to extend your thinking about it creatively by completing a group project. Your assignment is to compare scenes or characters from the play with fine art or photographic representations of those same scenes or characters. In carrying out this project, you will follow the steps below:

- Locate images that correspond to scenes or characters from the play.

- Organize and write commentary that compares and contrasts images with the written play.

- If resources allow, you can present your compare-and-contrast commentary and images as a slide show.

PART 1 Compare and Contrast Media

With a small group, find images that correspond to scenes or characters from *Romeo and Juliet*. Then write commentary in which you compare and contrast the images with the equivalent scenes and characters in the written play.

W.9–10.7

Find Images Conduct a search online or in print books (including your textbook) to find images that correspond to the play. You might wish to conduct a broad search first to see what types of images are available. Then narrow your findings to match particular scenes or characters in the play. Keep in mind that you should look for a variety of images, including fine art (paintings, sculptures, reliefs, etc.), photographs (stills from stage productions or movies), or cartoons. Here is a list of some characters and scenes you might wish to focus on:

- Romeo
- Juliet
- Mercutio
- Juliet's nurse
- Friar Laurence
- Romeo and Juliet's first meeting
- Romeo and Juliet's balcony scene
- Mercutio's death
- Romeo's killing of Tybalt
- The deaths of Romeo and Juliet

After you've found a reasonable number of images, go through them with your group and pick the ones that will work best for comparing and contrasting with the play.

RL.9–10.7 | **Organize Commentary** After you've chosen your images with your group, you'll need to plan and organize commentary that compares and contrasts the images with the equivalent characters and scenes in the written play. Use the chart below to compare and contrast your images with the text. Be sure to consider what is emphasized and absent in each medium.

Image/Corresponding Character or Scene in Text	Similarities	Differences

After you complete the chart, consider how you'd like to organize your images and commentary. Do you want to address one image at a time, or do you want to address all images related to one character or scene together? Keep in mind that your commentary and images are meant to be a part of a slide show. This means that the information and images need to flow together logically.

Write Commentary Decide which group members will be responsible for writing each part of the commentary. Use your similarities and differences chart to guide you as you write. Remember not to overload each slide with too much text. Include a title for your slide show and use bulleted lists and headings to make your commentary reader friendly.

After all the content is written, peer review each other's work and make sure it all flows together well and conveys the similarities and differences between the images and the written play. Remember to credit your image sources.

Present Your Commentary If you are not going on to Part 2 of the 21st Century Skills Project, your teacher may ask you to present your images and commentary as the end result of the project. You may also be evaluated on the presentation.

Present your commentary in a written or typed format that is visually appealing and presents the information clearly. Include print-outs of the necessary images and include them at point of use with your commentary. Once your group is satisfied that the content is presented effectively, turn it in to your teacher.

21st Century Skills Project

PART 2 Present a Slide Show

SL.9–10.5 After you've finished Part 1 of this project, create your slide show. Make sure your images and commentary are visually appealing, clearly presented, and flow together logically. Be sure to make strategic use of digital media to enhance understanding of your findings. In addition to your images and commentary, you may wish to include background music or sound effects.

Rehearse your slide show in front of friends or family members before presenting to your class. Make sure that each person in your group knows which portions of the presentation he or she is responsible for. As you rehearse, make sure the transitions between presenters are smooth.

After you've completed this project, answer the following questions.

1. How well does your slide show present the similarities and differences between the images and the written play?

_____

_____

_____

_____

_____

_____

_____

_____

2. Does your slide show flow well? Is information presented clearly? Explain your thoughts.

_____

_____

_____

_____

_____

_____

_____

_____

21st Century Skills Project

3. What would you change in the planning, creation, and presentation of this project if you were to do it again?

_____

_____

_____

_____

_____

_____

_____

_____

_____

_____

_____

Evaluate As you view your classmates' work, take notes about the content and effectiveness of their slide shows. Then use your notes to participate in a class discussion about the project.

1. Do the comparisons and contrasts of the images and the written play make sense? Explain your thoughts.

_____

_____

_____

_____

_____

_____

_____

_____

_____

21st Century Skills Project

2. Is the information in the slide show presented clearly and effectively? Explain your thoughts.

_____

_____

_____

_____

_____

_____

_____

_____

_____

_____

_____

3. What would you add or change in the slide show? Why? Consider content and organization.

_____

_____

_____

_____

_____

_____

_____

_____

_____

_____

_____

21st Century Skills Project

Group Discussion

from the Odyssey

Homer

Glencoe Literature, pages 834–898

RL.9–10.10 | Before starting the lesson, read the following selection and complete the lesson activities in ***Glencoe Literature.***

from the *Odyssey* (pages 834–898)

In this lesson you will analyze and discuss excerpts from Homer's *Odyssey.* You will then plan and create a multimedia exhibit exploring ancient Greek culture. Through your participation in the discussion and your work on the project, you will practice the following standards:

RL.9–10.2
RL.9–10.3

Key Ideas and Details

- Determine a theme or central idea of a text and analyze its development.
- Provide an objective summary of the text.
- Analyze how complex characters develop, interact with other characters, and advance the plot.

RL.9–10.6

Craft and Structure

- Analyze a cultural experience.

Group Discussion

Discussing epic poetry, such as Homer's *Odyssey,* within a small group can help you grow as a reader and as a member of a learning community. Together, you and other group members can arrive at a better understanding of a selection, its ideas and craft, and its connection to other works and areas of study.

PLAN

RL.9–10.1
W.9–10.9
W.9–10.9a
W.9–10.10
L.9–10.1
L.9–10.2
L.9–10.2c

To prepare for discussion, build your content knowledge by examining the selection in greater detail. On your own, write your answers to the questions that follow using text evidence. You may also write additional questions about the selection that you wish to discuss with your group. Your teacher may review your answers before the discussion, so be sure to use correct grammar, spelling, punctuation, and capitalization.

| RL.9–10.3 | **Character** A **character** is an individual in a work of fiction. **Flat characters** reveal only one personality trait. In contrast, **complex characters** are rich characters that possess many personality traits. An author may gradually reveal a character's full complexity over the course of a text. Paying attention to how each complex character interacts and develops will help you better appreciate the plot and theme of a literary work. |

1. Analyze the complexity of Odysseus as a character. Consider Odysseus's interactions with other characters and the traits he exhibits through these interactions. Cite evidence from the *Odyssey* to support your responses. Use the following chart to record your ideas. An example has been filled in for you.

Characters	Odysseus's Interactions with Other Characters	Odysseus's Traits	Evidence from the *Odyssey*
His crew	Odysseus tries to keep his men on course for Ithaca, but they face many perils.	Odysseus is an intelligent leader who cares about his crew.	"I carried wax along the line, and laid it/ thick on their ears." (Part 2, lines 43–44)
Cyclops (Part 1, lines 276–405)			
Telemachus (Parts 3 and 4)			
Antinous (Parts 3 and 4)			
Penelope's suitors (Part 4)			
Penelope (Part 4)			

RL.9–10.3 | **Motivation** is the stated or implied reason a character thinks, acts, or feels a certain way. Motivation may be an external circumstance, an internal moral or value, or an emotional impulse. Sometimes a character has multiple motivations that conflict with one another.

2. What is Odysseus's main motivation at the beginning of the epic poem? Does his motivation change during the course of his journey? Explain your thoughts.

_____

_____

_____

_____

_____

RL.9–10.2 | **Theme** A **theme** of a literary work is its message about life, the world, or human nature. Most works have an implied theme, which is revealed gradually through details of setting, character, and plot. A literary work may have more than one theme.

3. The theme(s) of a complex work, such as Homer's *Odyssey*, can often become clearer if you summarize the work first. Use the lines below to summarize the *Odyssey*. Remember that a summary only includes the main events and explains the main characters' problems and how they are resolved. Do not include personal opinions or comments.

_____

_____

_____

_____

_____

_____

_____

_____

4. What is the main theme of the *Odyssey*? What details support this theme? How does it develop over the course of the poem? Use the graphic organizer below to address these questions.

Main Theme		
Supporting Detail	**Supporting Detail**	**Supporting Detail**
How Theme Develops		

RL.9–10.6 **Cultural Experience** When you analyze the **cultural experience** reflected in a work of literature, you pay attention to details that reveal the setting, values, and behavior characteristic of a particular group of people at a particular point in time. Homer's *Odyssey* is among the world's oldest literary works, dating approximately to 800 B.C. It is both a literary treasure and an invaluable source of information about ancient Greek culture.

5. Review the actions of Zeus in Part 2, lines 272–351 and Athena in Part 3, lines 1–25. On the basis of these passages, what conclusions can you draw about the religious beliefs of the ancient Greeks?

_____

_____

_____

_____

_____

_____

_____

6. Reread the exchange between Odysseus and Telemachus in Part 3, lines 26–92. What view of family and family relationships does this passage suggest?

_____

_____

_____

_____

_____

_____

_____

7. Reread the exchange between Odysseus and Penelope in Part 4, lines 111–176. What do you learn about the Greeks' practice of marriage from this passage?

_____

_____

_____

_____

_____

_____

_____

8. Consider the length and difficulty of Odysseus's journey to Ithaca. What can you conclude about the Greeks' general opinion of sea voyages? Include details from the *Odyssey* to support your response.

_____

_____

_____

_____

_____

_____

ASSIGN

RL.9–10.2
RL.9–10.3
RL.9–10.6
SL.9–10.1
SL.9–10.1a

Meet with your literature group to plan your discussion. Each group member should become the expert on one or two of the questions answered on the previous pages. Each expert will then guide the discussion on his or her question(s). List each group member and the question(s) he or she will become an expert on in the following chart.

Group Member	Question(s) to Present

To become an expert on your question(s), spend some extra time thinking about your question(s) and consulting the text for relevant details. Building on your question(s), write down one or two discussion points or related questions for group members to consider as they explore text issues.

_____

_____

_____

_____

_____

_____

DISCUSS

SL.9–10.1
SL.9–10.1a
SL.9–10.1b
SL.9–10.1c
SL.9–10.1d

Break into your assigned literature group to conduct your discussion. The expert for question 1 should begin by reading aloud the question and leading the discussion in response. Follow this process for each question until you have covered them all.

Remember that literature groups contain room for disagreement. Healthy debate can help all members push their understanding to a new level. Use your time wisely so that you are able to discuss all the questions sufficiently.

In your discussion, follow the guidelines below.

Group Discussion

Discussion Guidelines

- Come to discussions prepared; be sure you have carefully and thoroughly answered all questions.

- Express your ideas clearly. When presenting on your question and commenting on others, support your ideas with concrete evidence from the text. Give specific page numbers.

- Work with your group to set rules for discussion and decision making (*e.g.,* informal consensus, taking votes on key issues, presenting alternative views).

- Work with your group to set clear goals and deadlines.

- Create individual roles as needed (*e.g.,* note taker, moderator, etc.).

- Propel conversations by posing and responding to questions that relate the current discussion to broader themes or larger ideas (*e.g.,* fantasy versus reality).

- Actively incorporate others into the discussion; clarify, verify, or challenge ideas and conclusions.

- Respond thoughtfully to diverse perspectives and summarize points of agreement and disagreement.

- Qualify or justify your views and understanding and make new connections in light of the evidence and reasoning presented.

At the end of your discussion, be prepared to share the insights you have gained with your class. On the lines below, briefly summarize the most interesting ideas or insights you heard or experienced during the discussion.

_____

_____

_____

_____

_____

from the Odyssey

Homer

21st Century Skills Project   Multimedia Exhibit

Now that you have analyzed and discussed the *Odyssey* in detail, you will have the opportunity to extend your thinking about it creatively by completing a group project. Your assignment is to develop a proposal for a multimedia exhibit that explores ancient Greek culture. In carrying out this project, you will follow the steps below:

- Conduct research about aspects of ancient Greek culture.
- Organize and write content for a multimedia exhibit proposal.
- If resources allow, you can create and present your multimedia exhibit.

PART 1 Develop a Proposal

With a small group, conduct research into various aspects of the Greek culture of Homer's age. Using the information you gather, develop a written proposal for a multimedia exhibit.

SL.9–10.2
W.9–10.6

Conduct Research Using reliable print and online resources, find information about the ancient Greeks. To help you get started, research aspects of ancient Greek culture that are mentioned in the excerpts from the *Odyssey* (one is filled in for you) and compile your notes in the chart on the next page.

Add notes to the chart about additional aspects of ancient Greek culture that you discover through your research. You might wish to address some or all of the following topics:

- religion
- heroism and leadership
- family relationships
- marriage
- hospitality
- revenge
- location of ancient Greece/geography
- seafaring traditions and practices
- oral poetic tradition

After you've completed the chart, answer the questions that follow to help focus your research.

Aspect of Ancient Greek Culture	Notes
Belief in ancient Greek gods and goddesses	

1. How did your research help you understand the actions of the characters in the *Odyssey*?

_____

_____

_____

_____

2. Which aspects of ancient Greek culture do you want to highlight in your multimedia exhibit? Why?

_____

_____

_____

_____

21st Century Skills Project

3 What main idea do you want to convey about the *Odyssey* and ancient Greek culture in your exhibit?

_____

_____

_____

_____

_____

RL.9–10.6 | **Organize Information** After you've finished conducting research, you'll need to organize the information that will go in your exhibit proposal with your group. Identify which aspects of ancient Greek culture you'll focus on in your proposal; what kinds of images, video, sound, or other media you'll include; and how these media will be arranged. As you plan your exhibit, it might help you to think of any museum exhibits you've seen. How were the images and artifacts arranged? By type? Chronologically? In some other way? Finally, think about how the information you've gathered helps you understand the cultural experience of the characters in the *Odyssey*. Use the graphic organizer below to help you organize your content.

Title of Exhibit	
Main Idea of Exhibit	

Aspect of Ancient Greek Culture	Supporting Media
Method of Media Organization	
Connection to the *Odyssey*	

Copyright © The McGraw-Hill Companies, Inc.

21ST Century Skills Project

Write Proposal Decide which group members will be responsible for writing each part of the proposal. Using the chart you filled out on page 66 as a guide, begin by explaining what the title and main idea of your exhibit will be. Then summarize the aspects of ancient Greek culture you will focus on, the important points you want to make about these aspects (including how they relate to the *Odyssey*), and which media you will use to support your points. Explain how the information in your exhibit will be organized.

After all the content is written, peer review each other's work and make sure it all flows together logically and supports the main idea you want to convey. Follow the citation guidelines on pages R35–R37 of your textbook to cite your sources.

Present Your Proposal If you are not going on to Part 2 of the 21st Century Skills Project, your teacher may ask you to present your proposal as the end result of the project. You may also be evaluated on the presentation.

Display your proposal in a written or typed format that is visually appealing and presents the information clearly. Include sample print-outs of the media you describe in your proposal. Once your group is satisfied that the content is presented effectively, turn it in to your teacher.

21st Century Skills Project

PART 2 Create a Multimedia Exhibit

SL.9–10.5

After you've finished Part 1 of this project, create your multimedia exhibit based on your proposal. With your group, decide how you will present your exhibit. Will you show everything in a slide show format? Or will some information be conveyed on handouts or in another manner?

SL.9–10.6

Make sure the information in your exhibit is visually appealing, clearly presented, and flows together logically. Be sure to make strategic use of digital media to enhance understanding of your findings. If you are using a slide show format, do not overload each slide with too much text. Make sure that images are interwoven with the text in a way that makes sense.

Rehearse your presentation in front of friends or family members before presenting to your class. Make sure that each person in your group knows which portions of the presentation he or she is responsible for. As you rehearse, make sure the transitions between presenters are smooth.

After you've completed this project, answer the following questions.

1. How well does your exhibit convey your main idea about the *Odyssey* and ancient Greek culture?

_____

_____

_____

_____

_____

_____

2. Does your exhibit help explain the cultural experience of the characters in the *Odyssey?* Explain your thoughts.

_____

_____

_____

_____

_____

21st Century Skills Project

3. Does your exhibit flow well? Is information presented clearly? Explain your thoughts.

_____

_____

_____

_____

_____

_____

4. What would you change in the planning, creation, and presentation of this project if you were to do it again?

_____

_____

_____

_____

_____

_____

Evaluate As you read and view your classmates' work, take notes about the content and effectiveness of their multimedia exhibits. Then use your notes to participate in a class discussion about the project.

1. Does the main idea about the *Odyssey* and ancient Greek culture make sense? Is it adequately supported? Explain your thoughts.

_____

_____

_____

_____

_____

_____

21st Century Skills Project

2. Does the exhibit help explain the cultural experience of the characters in the *Odyssey?* Explain your thoughts.

_____

_____

_____

_____

_____

_____

3. Is the information in the exhibit presented clearly and effectively? Explain your thoughts.

_____

_____

_____

_____

_____

_____

4. What would you add or change in the exhibit? Why? Consider content and organization.

_____

_____

_____

_____

_____

_____

21st Century Skills Project

Reading Lessons: Informational Text

Escape from Afghanistan

Farah Ahmedi

Glencoe Literature, pages 307–317

RI.9–10.10 Before starting the lesson, read the following selection and complete the lesson activities in **Glencoe Literature.**

"Escape from Afghanistan" **(pages 307–317)**

In this lesson you will analyze and discuss Farah Ahmedi's autobiography "Escape from Afghanistan." You will then write an autobiographical narrative that you can publish online. Through your participation in the discussion and your work on the project, you will practice the following standards:

RI.9–10.3 **Key Ideas and Details**

- Analyze how the author unfolds a series of events, including the order in which the points are made, how they are introduced and developed, and the connections between them.

RI.9–10.4
RI.9–10.6 **Craft and Structure**

- Determine the meaning of words and phrases as they are used in a text.
- Analyze the cumulative impact of specific word choices on meaning and tone.
- Determine an author's purpose in a text.

Group Discussion

Discussing an autobiography, such as "Escape from Afghanistan," within a small group can help you grow as a reader and as a member of a learning community. Together, you and other group members can arrive at a better understanding of a selection, its ideas and craft, and its connection to other works and areas of study.

PLAN

RI.9–10.1
W.9–10.9
W.9–10.9b
W.9–10.10
L.9–10.1
L.9–10.2
L.9–10.2c
To prepare for discussion, build your content knowledge by examining the selection in greater detail. On your own, write your answers to the questions that follow using text evidence. You may also write additional questions about the selection that you wish to discuss with your group. Your teacher may review your answers before the discussion, so be sure to use correct grammar, spelling, punctuation, and capitalization.

Group Discussion

RI.9–10.3 **Key Events** Farah Ahmedi's "Escape from Afghanistan" is an example of **autobiography,** or an author's account of his or her own life. In an autobiography, the author typically focuses on the key events and people that have shaped his or her experiences. Most autobiographies are told from the first-person point of view and present events in chronological order.

1. The chart below contains the key events from "Escape from Afghanistan" in the order in which Farah Ahmedi presents them. Explain how each event is developed through facts, explanations, or other details. An example has been completed for you.

Key Event	How Event Is Developed
Ahmedi and her mother receive a letter from a distant cousin, urging them to leave Kabul, Afghanistan, and come to her home in Quetta, Pakistan.	Ahmedi develops this event by providing passages from the actual letter and details about her cousin's life in Quetta.
Ahmedi and her mother decide to leave Kabul and make a plan for their escape.	
Ahmedi and her mother travel from Kabul to Jalalabad by bus.	
Ahmedi and her mother travel from Jalalabad to the Afghanistan border by van.	
Ahmedi and her mother arrive at the border gate but are unable to pass through it. They must spend the night out in the open.	
Ahmedi and her mother meet Ghulam Ali and his family and travel with them across a mountain range on a smugglers' path into Pakistan.	
Ahmedi, her mother, and the family of Ghulam Ali successfully climb the mountains and arrive in Pakistan.	

Group Discussion

2. Identify the various hardships that Ahmedi and her mother face during their escape from Afghanistan. What connections does Ahmedi make between these circumstances and those of other people they meet along the way? Support your answer with details from the text.

_____

_____

_____

_____

_____

3. **Transitions** are connecting words and phrases, such as *first, next, therefore,* or *as a result,* used by an author to indicate a relationship between ideas. Reread the first full paragraph on page 313. What transitions does Ahmedi use in this paragraph? How do these transitions help connect the events in this paragraph to the ones in the preceding paragraph?

_____

_____

_____

_____

_____

RI.9–10.6 **Author's Purpose** An author's intent in writing a work is called an **author's purpose.** Authors typically write for one or more of the following purposes: to persuade, to inform, to explain, to entertain, or to describe. You can often determine an author's purpose by examining his or her presentation of key events and people.

4. What do you think Farah Ahmedi's purpose was in writing "Escape from Afghanistan"? How can you tell?

_____

_____

_____

_____

_____

Group Discussion

Name_____ Class_____ Date_____

RI.9–10.4 **Imagery** is descriptive language that appeals to one or more of the five senses: sight, hearing, touch, taste, and smell. Imagery helps create an emotional response in the reader.

5. In the chart below, list examples of imagery from "Escape to Afghanistan" that appeal to the five senses. Give one example for each sense. Then explain what each example means.

Sense	Example of Imagery	Meaning
Sight		
Hearing		
Touch		
Taste		
Smell		

RI.9–10.4 **Tone** An author's attitude toward his or her subject is called **tone.** It is conveyed through an author's choice of words and details, including his or her use of imagery. A writer's tone may be described in a variety of ways, such as sympathetic, serious, ironic, sad, bitter, and so on.

6. How would you describe the tone of "Escape from Afghanistan"? How do the Ahmedi's specific word choices throughout the selection reveal her tone? Cite examples from the autobiography to support your answer.

_____

_____

_____

_____

_____

ASSIGN

RI.9–10.3
RI.9–10.4
RI.9–10.6
SL.9–10.1
SL.9–10.1a

Meet with your literature group to plan your discussion. Each group member should become the expert on one or more of the questions answered on the previous pages. Each expert will then guide the discussion on his or her question(s). List each group member and the question(s) he or she will become an expert on in the chart below.

Group Member	Question(s) to Present

To become an expert on your question(s), spend some extra time thinking about your question(s) and consulting the text for relevant details. Building on your question(s), write down one or two discussion points or related questions for group members to consider as they explore text issues.

_____

_____

_____

_____

DISCUSS

SL.9–10.1
SL.9–10.1a
SL.9–10.1b
SL.9–10.1c
SL.9–10.1d

Break into your assigned literature group to conduct your discussion. The expert for question 1 should begin by reading aloud the question and leading the discussion in response. Follow this process for each question until you have covered them all.

Remember that literature groups contain room for disagreement. Healthy debate can help all members push their understanding to a new level. Use your time wisely so that you are able to discuss all the questions sufficiently.

In your discussion, follow the guidelines below.

Discussion Guidelines

- Come to discussions prepared; be sure you have carefully and thoroughly answered all questions.

- Express your ideas clearly. When presenting on your question and commenting on others, support your ideas with concrete evidence from the text. Give specific page numbers.

- Work with your group to set rules for discussion and decision making (*e.g.,* informal consensus, taking votes on key issues, presenting alternative views).

- Work with your group to set clear goals and deadlines.

- Create individual roles as needed (*e.g.,* note taker, moderator, etc.).

- Propel conversations by posing and responding to questions that relate the current discussion to broader themes or larger ideas (*e.g.,* fantasy versus reality).

- Actively incorporate others into the discussion; clarify, verify, or challenge ideas and conclusions.

- Respond thoughtfully to diverse perspectives and summarize points of agreement and disagreement.

- Qualify or justify your views and understanding and make new connections in light of the evidence and reasoning presented.

At the end of your discussion, be prepared to share the insights you have gained with your class. On the lines below, briefly summarize the most interesting ideas or insights you heard or experienced during the discussion.

_____

_____

_____

_____

_____

Escape from Afghanistan
Farah Ahmedi

21st Century Skills Project Multimedia Narrative

Now that you have analyzed and discussed the autobiography in detail, you will have the opportunity to extend your thinking about it creatively by completing a project. Your assignment is to write an autobiographical narrative. If resources allow, you can publish your autobiographical narrative online.

PART 1 Write an Autobiographical Narrative

Farah Ahmedi's "Escape from Afghanistan" is a story of survival against all odds. Write an autobiographical narrative about a time in your life when you faced and overcame an obstacle or a series of obstacles.

W.9–10.3
W.9–10.3a

Plan Your Narrative First, choose a relevant incident from your own life. Next, identify the main conflict and key events of the incident on the lines below. Focus on events that relate to the main idea you want to convey about your experience. Sequence these events in the graphic organizer on the next page so that your narrative will have a smooth progression of events that build on one another to create a coherent whole.

Main Conflict: _____

_____

_____

_____

_____

_____

_____

_____

_____

_____

_____

Event:

↓

Event:

↓

Event:

↓

Event:

↓

Event:

↓

Event:

↓

Event:

21st Century Skills Project

W.9–10.3
W.9–10.3a
W.9–10.3b
W.9–10.3c
W.9–10.3d
W.9–10.3e

Draft Your Narrative Using your events chart to guide you, draft your narrative. As you write, keep the following tips in mind:

- Engage and orient the reader by establishing the problem or situation and introducing yourself as the narrator.

- Use narrative techniques such as dialogue, pacing, description, and reflection to develop the experience and events.

- Use specific details to shape the development of your main idea about facing and overcoming an obstacle.

- Use precise words and phrases, telling details, and sensory language to convey a vivid picture of your experience for your reader.

- Provide a conclusion that follows from and reflects on what you have experienced.

W.9–10.4

Conduct a Peer Review After you're finished writing your narrative, exchange it with a partner to conduct a peer review. Use the following checklist to guide your review.

☐ Are the development, organization, and style appropriate to the purpose and audience?

☐ Does the narrative explore an incident in which the narrator faced and overcame an obstacle or a series of obstacles?

☐ Is the main idea of the narrative clear?

☐ Do the events build on one another to create a coherent whole?

☐ Does the writer use narrative techniques to develop the experience?

☐ Is the narrative free of errors in spelling, grammar, and mechanics?

Present Your Narrative If you are not going on to Part 2 of the 21st Century Skills Project, your teacher may ask you to present your narrative as the end result of the project. You may also be evaluated on the presentation.

Once you have made any necessary revisions to your narrative, write or type it in a neat and legible format and turn it in to your teacher.

21st Century Skills Project

PART 2 Publish Online

SL.9–10.5 After you've finished Part 1 of this project, publish your autobiographical narrative online in an interactive format that includes hyperlinks to images and other visual media (such as personal photographs or video clips).

Links to Visual Media When you publish your autobiographical narrative, you will include hyperlinks to visual media, which will elaborate on the images and details you've included in your account. These links will help your readers get a better understanding of the subject you wrote about. For example, if you're writing about a time you overcame stage fright, you might want to include a photograph or two from your successful performance.

Before you publish your autobiographical narrative, fill in the chart below to help you decide what details and/or other media you want to link to. If necessary, you may add boxes for extra images.

Image/Detail in Autobiographical Narrative	Line Number(s)	Corresponding Visual Media Link

21st Century Skills Project

W.9–10.6 | **Publish and Present** After you've completed your chart, decide where you will publish your autobiographical narrative. If your school already has a Web site for student work, you might consider publishing your account there. You can also search online for Web sites that allow you to create your own page for free. These types of sites often provide templates and are easy to use.

Publish your autobiographical narrative on your chosen site. Using your chart as a guide, hyperlink various images in your account to photos, video clips, and other media. When you're finished, send the URL of your site to your teacher and classmates so they can read and view your work.

After you've completed this project, answer the following questions.

1. Does your autobiographical narrative clearly identify an experience of facing and overcoming an obstacle? Is it presented effectively without unnecessary details? Explain your thoughts.

_____

_____

_____

_____

2. Which images in your autobiography are particularly helpful? Why?

_____

_____

_____

_____

_____

3. What would you change in the planning, creation, and presentation of this project if you were to do it again?

_____

_____

_____

_____

_____

21st Century Skills Project

Evaluate Read your classmates' autobiographical narratives once without clicking on any of the links so that you understand the content of these accounts. Then read the autobiographical narratives a second time and click on the links to see the media. As you read and view your classmates' work, take notes about the content and effectiveness of their written work and visual media. Then use your notes to participate in a class discussion about the project.

1. How well does the autobiographical narrative convey the author's experience of facing and overcoming an obstacle? Is the experience presented clearly and effectively? Explain your thoughts.

_____

_____

_____

_____

_____

2. How well do the links to visual media connect to images/details in the autobiographical narrative? Explain your thoughts.

_____

_____

_____

_____

3. What would you add or change in the autobiographical narrative or the accompanying visual media? Why?

_____

_____

_____

_____

21st Century Skills Project

Walking

Linda Hogan

Glencoe Literature, pages 340–346

RI.9–10.10 | Before starting the lesson, read the following selection and complete the lesson activities in *Glencoe Literature.*

"Walking" (pages 340–346)

In this lesson you will analyze and discuss Linda Hogan's descriptive essay "Walking." You will then plan and create a blog in which you record regular observations about an aspect of nature, such as those Hogan includes in her essay. Through your participation in the discussion and your work on the project, you will practice the following standards:

RI.9–10.2 | **Key Ideas and Details**
- Determine a central idea of a text.
- Provide a summary of a text.

RI.9–10.4
RI.9–10.5 | **Craft and Structure**
- Determine the meaning of words and phrases, including figurative and connotative meanings.
- Analyze the cumulative impact of specific word choices on meaning and tone.
- Analyze in detail how an author's ideas are developed by a text.

Group Discussion

Discussing an essay, such as "Walking," within a small group can help you grow as a reader and as a member of a learning community. Together, you and other group members can arrive at a better understanding of a selection, its ideas and craft, and its connection to other works and areas of study.

PLAN

RI.9–10.1
W.9–10.9
W.9–10.9b
W.9–10.10
L.9–10.1
L.9–10.2
L.9–10.2c | To prepare for discussion, build your content knowledge by examining the selection in greater detail. On your own, write your answers to the questions that follow using text evidence. You may also write additional questions about the selection that you wish to discuss with your group. Your teacher may review your answers before the discussion, so be sure to use correct grammar, spelling, punctuation, and capitalization.

| RI.9–10.2 |
| RI.9–10.5 |

Main Idea The central, controlling idea in an informational text is called the **main idea.** Main ideas are usually supported and refined by specific details. Sometimes a text has more than one main idea.

1. A text's main idea(s) can often become clearer if you summarize the text first. Use the lines below to summarize "Walking." Remember that a summary only includes the main points. Do not include personal opinions or comments.

_____

_____

_____

_____

_____

_____

_____

_____

_____

_____

2. What do you think the main idea of the selection is? What particular sentences, paragraphs, or larger sections of text help develop this idea? How does it develop over the course of the text? Use the graphic organizer below to address these questions.

Main Idea:		
Supporting Text:	**Supporting Text:**	**Supporting Text:**
How Main Idea Develops:		

RI.9–10.4
L.9–10.4
L.9–10.4c
L.9–10.5
L.9–10.5b

Denotation and Connotation The **denotation** of a word refers to its literal definition, or its meaning in a dictionary. The **connotation** of a word refers to the attitudes or feelings associated with it. For example, both *brilliance* and *glare* may be defined as "excessively bright," but *glare* has a negative connotation that *brilliance* does not. A word may carry a negative, neutral, or positive connotation.

Place the words in each group on a continuum to show the positive, neutral, or negative connotations associated with each word. Then on the lines given, explain the shared denotation of the words and their different connotations. You may use print or electronic resources, such as a dictionary or thesaurus, to help you in your work. An example has been completed for you.

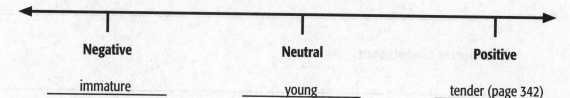

Negative	Neutral	Positive
immature	young	tender (page 342)

Shared Denotation:
having lived for a short time; in the early part of life or growth.

Different Connotations:
"Immature" has negative connotations associated with underdevelopment, childishness, and foolishness. "Young" is neutral. "Tender" has positive associations with something that is delicate and gentle.

3.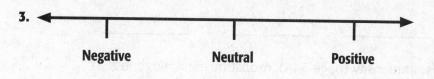

Negative	Neutral	Positive

Words: mysterious (page 343), strange, unexplained

Shared Denotation:

_____

_____

Different Connotations:

_____

_____

_____

_____

Group Discussion

4.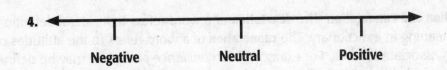

Negative   Neutral   Positive

_____   _____   _____

Words: faded (page 343), pale, lightened

Shared Denotation:

_____

_____

Different Connotations:

_____

_____

_____

_____

5.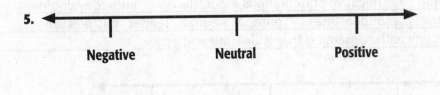

Negative   Neutral   Positive

_____   _____   _____

Words: immensity (page 344), monstrousness, largeness

Shared Denotation:

_____

_____

Different Connotations:

_____

_____

_____

_____

Group Discussion

RI.9–10.4
L.9–10.5
L.9–10.5a

Figurative Language In literature, **figurative language** is language used for descriptive effect, often to imply meaning. Expressions of figurative language are not literally true but express some truth beyond the literal level. Types of figurative language include personification, similes, and metaphors.

6. A **metaphor** is a comparison between two unlike things. In a metaphor, the comparison is implied rather than stated. There is no use of connective words such as *like* or *as*. Reread the first paragraph of "Walking" on page 342. Identify three metaphors Hogan uses to describe the sunflower. What do you learn about the sunflower through these metaphors?

_____

_____

_____

_____

_____

7. **Personification** is a figure of speech in which human qualities are attributed to a nonhuman thing. Identify three examples of personification in paragraphs 7–9 on page 343. What types of things does Hogan personify in these paragraphs?

_____

_____

_____

_____

_____

8. What do you think Hogan is trying to say through her use of personification?

_____

_____

_____

_____

_____

_____

Group Discussion

RI.9–10.4 **Imagery** is descriptive language that appeals to one or more of the five senses: sight, hearing, touch, taste, and smell. Imagery helps create an emotional response in the reader.

9. In the chart below, list examples of imagery from "Walking" that appeal to the five senses. Give one example for each sense. Then explain what each example means.

Sense	Example of Imagery	Meaning
Sight		
Hearing		
Touch		
Taste		
Smell		

RI.9–10.4 **Tone** An author's attitude toward his or her subject is called **tone**. It is conveyed through an author's choice of words and details, including his or her use of figurative language and imagery. A writer's tone may be described in a variety of ways, such as sympathetic, serious, ironic, sad, bitter, and so on.

10. How would you describe the tone of "Walking"? How do Hogan's specific word choices reveal her tone? Cite examples from the essay to support your answer.

_____

_____

_____

_____

_____

Group Discussion

ASSIGN

RI.9–10.2
RI.9–10.4
RI.9–10.5
SL.9–10.1
SL.9–10.1a

Meet with your literature group to plan your discussion. Each group member should become an expert for one or more of the questions answered on the previous pages. Each expert will then guide the discussion on his or her question(s). List each group member and the question(s) he or she will become an expert on in the chart below.

Group Member	Question(s) to Present

To become an expert on your question(s), spend some extra time thinking about your question(s) and consulting the text for relevant details. Building on your question(s), write down one or two discussion points or related questions for group members to consider as they explore text issues.

_____

_____

_____

_____

_____

_____

DISCUSS

SL.9–10.1
SL.9–10.1a
SL.9–10.1b
SL.9–10.1c
SL.9–10.1d

Break into your assigned literature group to conduct your discussion. The expert for question 1 should begin by reading aloud the question and leading the discussion in response. Follow this process for each question until you have covered them all.

Remember that literature groups contain room for disagreement. Healthy debate can help all members push their understanding to a new level. Use your time wisely so that you are able to discuss all the questions sufficiently.

In your discussion, follow the guidelines below.

Discussion Guidelines
• Come to discussions prepared; be sure you have carefully and thoroughly answered all questions.
• Express your ideas clearly. When presenting on your question and commenting on others, support your ideas with concrete evidence from the text. Give specific page numbers.
• Work with your group to set rules for discussion and decision making (*e.g.,* informal consensus, taking votes on key issues, presenting alternative views).
• Work with your group to set clear goals and deadlines.
• Create individual roles as needed (*e.g.,* note taker, moderator, etc.).
• Propel conversations by posing and responding to questions that relate the current discussion to broader themes or larger ideas (*e.g.,* fantasy versus reality).
• Actively incorporate others into the discussion; clarify, verify, or challenge ideas and conclusions.
• Respond thoughtfully to diverse perspectives and summarize points of agreement and disagreement.
• Qualify or justify your views and understanding and make new connections in light of the evidence and reasoning presented.

At the end of your discussion, be prepared to share the insights you have gained with your class. On the lines below, briefly summarize the most interesting ideas or insights you heard or experienced during the discussion.

_____

_____

_____

_____

_____

Group Discussion

Walking

Linda Hogan

> ### 21st Century Skills Project Blog
>
> Now that you have analyzed and discussed the descriptive essay in detail, you will have the opportunity to extend your thinking about it creatively by completing a project. Your assignment is to plan and create a blog in which you record regular observations about an aspect of nature, such as those Linda Hogan includes in "Walking." In carrying out this project, you will follow the steps below:
>
> - Select an aspect of nature that you want to focus on.
> - Plan the overall structure of your nature blog.
> - Organize and write content for blog entries.
> - If resources allow, you can build your blog on the Internet.

PART 1 Write Nature Blog Entries

In "Walking," Linda Hogan describes her nature walks and explains a life lesson she learned from closely watching the growth of a sunflower over the course of a summer.

Hogan concludes that nature has a language of its own that humans can hear if they take the time to listen to their surroundings. In this lesson, you will write blog entries based on your observations of an aspect of nature. Then, you will use your work to draw a conclusion about the relationship between humans and the natural world.

Choose Your Subject First, choose an aspect of nature that you wish to focus on and carefully observe as your subject during a period of about two weeks. Your selection should involve something that really sparks your interest and that you can experience easily and directly—such as a gnarled tree within your neighborhood, ducks or other animals at a local pond, or the sun setting in the evening sky.

Schedule Observations After you've completed this first step, you will need to figure out when to observe your subject and for how long. Remember that you want to spend enough time to make meaningful observations. Ideally, you should observe your subject at least four separate times.

RI.9–10.4
L.9–10.5
L.9–10.5a

Take Notes Next, you'll want to turn your attention to making your observations and taking detailed notes. Like Linda Hogan, you will want to use figurative language and imagery to bring your experiences to life for your readers.

Use the graphic organizer below to help you organize your thoughts as you make each of your observations.

Date: _____

Time: _____

Subject: _____

Key Details: _____

_____

_____

Figurative Language or Imagery That Comes to Mind: _____

_____

_____

Changes Since Last Observation: _____

_____

_____

Tone, or Attitude, Toward Subject: _____

_____

_____

RI.9–10.4

Draft Blog Entries After you have completed each observation, you will need to write a blog entry. Use the observation notes that you have recorded to help you in this process. Each blog entry should summarize your experience.

As you write each blog entry, keep the following tips in mind:

- Identify the time, place, and subject of your observation within the first sentence or two of your entry.
- Choose your words carefully. Use vivid figurative language and imagery to help you communicate your experiences.

21st Century Skills Project

- Convey your ideas as precisely as possible and avoid unnecessary words.
- Use complete sentences and proper grammar and punctuation.

You may wish to enhance your entries by including hyperlinks to visual media, such as photographs, fine art images, or Web pages. If you decide to include such hyperlinks in your work, you'll need to determine where they should appear within your entries. Use the chart below to compile this information.

Link Needed	Location of Link in Content

Draft Final Statement Once you have written all of your blog entries, you will need to create a final statement that explains what you have learned about life from your observations. You'll want to focus on drawing a general conclusion about the relationship between humans and the natural world.

Present Your Blog Entries If you are not going on to Part 2 of the 21st Century Skills Project, your teacher may ask you to present your blog entries and final statement as the end result of the project. You may also be evaluated on the presentation.

Display your work in a written or typed format that is neat and clearly organized. If you have plans to include hyperlinks, indicate where these would appear by underlining the relevant text to be linked and including footnotes that summarize what each link is about. You could also include sample print-outs of the links and number them to match your footnotes.

21st Century Skills Project

PART 2 Build a Nature Blog

SL.9–10.5 After you've finished Part 1 of this project, build a blog for your content. There are many sites that will allow you to create your own blog for free. These types of sites often provide templates and are easy to use.

You'll need to establish a title for your blog, a general page design, and a label for each blog entry. Also, you'll need to confirm the total number of blog entries and any hyperlinks to visual media. Make sure the information on your blog is visually appealing, clearly presented, and easy to navigate. You might wish to consult existing blogs about nature, such as those sponsored by the National Park Service and the Sierra Club, to get ideas.

Answer the questions below to help you organize your thoughts about the structure of your blog.

Questions About Blog Structure	My Answers
1. The title of my blog should catch my readers' attention and relate to my subject matter. What will I call my blog?	
2. The general design of my blog should be eye-catching yet not overwhelming. What main design element will I use to engage my readers (*e.g.* pieces of clip art, a background photograph, a bold font color, a large font size, etc.)?	
3. My blog should contain at least four separate entries based on my observations. How many total entries will my blog have? What labels will I use for my entries?	
4. My blog entries may be enhanced by including hyperlinks to photographs of my subject matter or other images. What, if any, images have I chosen to include? How will these images help my readers understand my entries?	

21st Century Skills Project

After you've completed this project, answer the following questions.

1. How well does the content of your blog entries convey your experiences of nature? Explain your thoughts.

_____

_____

_____

_____

_____

2. Does your blog have an appealing design that complements its content? Is information presented clearly? Explain your thoughts.

_____

_____

_____

_____

3. If you have included hyperlinks to visual media, are they closely related to your content?

_____

_____

_____

_____

4. What would you change in the planning, creation, and presentation of this project if you were to do it again?

_____

_____

_____

_____

21st Century Skills Project

Evaluate As you read and view your classmates' work, take notes about the content and effectiveness of their blog entries. Then use your notes to participate in a class discussion about the project.

1. Do the blog entries include effective examples of figurative language or imagery? Explain your thoughts.

_____

_____

_____

_____

2. Does the design of the blog complement its content? Is the information within the blog entries presented clearly? Explain your thoughts.

_____

_____

_____

_____

3. If hyperlinks to visual media appear, do they help you to understand the student's experiences?

_____

_____

_____

_____

4. What would you add or change to the blog? Why? Consider design and content.

_____

_____

_____

_____

21st Century Skills Project

from Into Thin Air

Jon Krakauer

Glencoe Literature, pages 355–368

RI.9–10.10 Before starting the lesson, read the following selection and complete the lesson activities in *Glencoe Literature.*

from Into Thin Air **(pages 355–368)**

In this lesson you will analyze and discuss an excerpt from Jon Krakauer's *Into Thin Air*. You will then plan and create a Web page that explores various accounts of the tragic events of May 11, 1996, on Mount Everest. Through your participation in the discussion and your work on the project, you will practice the following standards:

RI.9–10.2 | **Key Ideas and Details**
- Determine a central idea of a text.
- Provide an objective summary of the text.

RI.9–10.4
RI.9–10.5
RI.9–10.6 | **Craft and Structure**
- Determine the meaning of words and phrases, including technical meanings.
- Analyze how an author's ideas are developed by text.
- Determine an author's point of view or purpose in a text.

RI.9–10.7 | **Integration of Knowledge and Ideas**
- Analyze accounts of a subject told in different mediums.

Group Discussion

Discussing nonfiction, such as *Into Thin Air*, within a small group can help you grow as a reader and as a member of a learning community. Together, you and other group members can arrive at a better understanding of a selection, its ideas and craft, and its connection to other works and areas of study.

PLAN

RI.9–10.1
W.9–10.9
W.9–10.9b
W.9–10.10
L.9–10.1
L.9–10.2
L.9–10.2c | To prepare for discussion, build your content knowledge by examining the selection in greater detail. On your own, write your answers to the questions that follow using text evidence. You may also write additional questions about the selection that you wish to discuss with your group. Your teacher may review your answers before the discussion, so be sure to use correct grammar, spelling, punctuation, and capitalization.

Group Discussion

RI.9–10.2
RI.9–10.5

Main Idea The central, controlling idea in an informational text is called the **main idea.** Main ideas are usually supported and refined by specific details. Sometimes a text has more than one main idea.

1. A text's main idea(s) can often become clearer if you summarize the text first. Use the lines below to summarize the excerpt from *Into Thin Air*. Remember that a summary only includes the main points. Do not include personal opinions or comments.

_____

_____

_____

_____

_____

_____

_____

_____

2. What do you think the main idea of the excerpt is? What particular sentences, paragraphs, or larger sections of text help develop this idea? How does it develop over the course of the excerpt? Use the graphic organizer below to address these questions.

Main Idea:		
Supporting Text:	**Supporting Text:**	**Supporting Text:**
How Main Idea Develops:		

RI.9–10.6 | **Author's Purpose** An author's intent in writing a work is called an **author's purpose.** Authors typically write for one or more of the following purposes: to persuade, to inform, to explain, to entertain, or to describe.

3. What do you think Jon Krakauer's primary purpose was in writing *Into Thin Air*? Explain your thoughts.

_____

_____

_____

RI.9–10.6 | **Author's Perspective** The combination of experiences, values, and ideas that shape the way an author looks at the world or at a particular subject is called the **author's perspective.**

4. What perspective of mountain climbing does Jon Krakauer reveal in *Into Thin Air*? Support your response with details from the selection.

_____

_____

_____

_____

RI.9–10.7 | **Accounts Across Mediums** Accounts of a subject, such as the deadly storm of May 11, 1996, on Mount Everest, may be found in different **mediums,** or modes of expression, such as memoirs, newspapers, Web sites, or films. When you compare accounts of a subject across different mediums, you determine which details are emphasized in each account.

5. Examine the photograph on page 359 of your textbook. Which details of the Mount Everest expedition are emphasized in the photograph? Which details are emphasized in Jon Krakauer's account of the climb?

_____

_____

_____

_____

_____

Group Discussion

RI.9–10.4 **Technical Language** Language that is specialized or particular to a certain sport, hobby, or field is called **technical language.** Some technical language may only have meaning within a certain profession (for example, musicians use the term *score* to describe the written form of a musical work), while other technical language may be familiar to the general public (such as the cooking term *marinate*, which means "to soak in a flavored liquid").

6. *Into Thin Air* contains many technical terms related to the sport of mountain climbing. Four examples of these specialized words appear below. What does each term mean? Why has the writer chosen to use each term? Consult a print or an online dictionary, if necessary. Use the chart below to record your answers. An example has been completed for you.

Word	Meaning	Why the Word Is Used
crampons (page 366)	Steel spikes attached to boots to prevent sliding on ice or snow	Krakauer uses crampons to descend icy, steep slopes.
regulator *n.* (page 358)		
hypoxia *n.* (page 361)		
cornice *n.* (page 361)		
rappel *v.* (page 364)		

ASSIGN

RI.9–10.2
RI.9–10.4
RI.9–10.5
RI.9–10.6
RI.9–10.7
SL.9–10.1
SL.9–10.1a

Meet with your literature group to plan your discussion. Each group member should become an expert on one or more of the questions answered on the previous pages. Each expert will then guide the discussion on his or her question(s). List each group member and the question(s) he or she will become an expert on in the chart below.

Group Member	Question(s) to Present

To become an expert on your question(s), spend some extra time thinking about your question(s) and consulting the text for relevant details. Building on your question(s), write down one or two discussion points or related questions for group members to consider as they explore text issues.

_____

_____

_____

_____

_____

_____

Group Discussion

DISCUSS

SL.9–10.1
SL.9–10.1a
SL.9–10.1b
SL.9–10.1c
SL.9–10.1d

Break into your assigned literature group to conduct your discussion. The expert for question 1 should begin by reading aloud the question and leading the discussion in response. Follow this process for each question until you have covered them all.

Remember that literature groups contain room for disagreement. Healthy debate can help all members push their understanding to a new level. Use your time wisely so that you are able to discuss all the questions sufficiently.

In your discussion, follow the guidelines below.

Discussion Guidelines

- Come to discussions prepared; be sure you have carefully and thoroughly answered all questions.

- Express your ideas clearly. When presenting on your question and commenting on others, support your ideas with concrete evidence from the text. Give specific page numbers.

- Work with your group to set rules for discussion and decision making (*e.g.,* informal consensus, taking votes on key issues, presenting alternative views).

- Work with your group to set clear goals and deadlines.

- Create individual roles as needed (*e.g.,* note taker, moderator, etc.).

- Propel conversations by posing and responding to questions that relate the current discussion to broader themes or larger ideas (*e.g.,* fantasy versus reality).

- Actively incorporate others into the discussion; clarify, verify, or challenge ideas and conclusions.

- Respond thoughtfully to diverse perspectives and summarize points of agreement and disagreement.

- Qualify or justify your views and understanding and make new connections in light of the evidence and reasoning presented.

At the end of your discussion, be prepared to share the insights you have gained with your class. On the lines below, briefly summarize the most interesting ideas or insights you heard or experienced during the discussion.

_____

_____

_____

_____

_____

from Into Thin Air

Jon Krakauer

21ˢᵗ Century Skills Project   Web Page

Now that you have analyzed and discussed the excerpt from *Into Thin Air* in detail, you will have the opportunity to extend your thinking about it creatively by completing a group project. Your assignment is to develop content for a Web page that compares Jon Krakauer's memoir with other accounts of the Mount Everest disaster. In carrying out this project, you will follow the steps below:

- Locate accounts of the deadly storm on Mount Everest as told in different mediums.
- Organize and write content for a Web page.
- If resources allow, you can build your Web page on the Internet.

PART 1 Develop Content for a Web Page

With a small group, find accounts in different mediums of the tragic events of May 11, 1996. Locate the accounts in print sources (books, newspapers, magazines), Web sites, photographs, TV news accounts, documentaries, and/ or dramatic films. Then, analyze the accounts to determine what details of the Mount Everest disaster they emphasize.

SL.9–10.2
W.9–10.7

Conduct Research Using reliable print and online resources, find images and accounts of the disaster. You might wish to conduct a broad search first to see what kinds of accounts are available. Then, narrow your findings to accounts that mirror particular people, scenes, or issues in *Into Thin Air*. Additionally, you might consider obtaining a copy of *Into Thin Air: Death on Everest,* a 1997 film adaptation of Krakauer's memoir. You might also wish to consult works by mountaineer David Breashears, most notably his documentary films *Everest* and *Storm Over Everest* and *Everest: Mountain Without Mercy,* a photographic account of the disaster. Another source that may be of interest is *The Climb,* the memoir of Anatoli Boukreev, the lead guide of Scott Fischer's Mountain Madness expedition. Remember to evaluate the credibility and accuracy of each source.

After you've found a reasonable number of accounts from different mediums, go through them with your group and pick the ones that will work best for comparing and contrasting with *Into Thin Air*.

RI.9–10.7 | **Compare and Contrast Accounts** After you've chosen your accounts with your group, you'll need to plan your comparison of people, scenes, and issues in the accounts with the equivalent people, scenes, and issues in Krakauer's memoir. Use the chart below to compare and contrast the details emphasized in each account.

Account and Medium	Similarities in Details Emphasized	Differences in Details Emphasized
Into Thin Air, memoir		

After you've completed your chart, consider the unique insights contained within each individual account.

- What are the insights of the accounts?
- How do different mediums lend themselves to different kinds of insights?
- Taken together, how do the different accounts combine to help you reach a fuller understanding of the Mount Everest disaster?

Consider how the main ideas in other accounts reflect or differ from the main idea of *Into Thin Air*. Then, develop a main idea about the Mount Everest disaster as presented in different mediums.

RI.9–10.2

Organize Information After you've finished researching accounts, you'll need to organize and write the content for your Web page. You'll also need to determine what the navigation features of the Web page should be and whether any hyperlinks to other media, such as maps, photographs, and film clips, will be included. Consider how you'd like to present each account: with printouts of images? Time lines? Screen shots? Decide if you want to address one account at a time, or instead organize your Web page according to events or issues that feature in all the accounts.

Finally, think about how you will illustrate the different emphases in the accounts, and how you will help viewers to understand the accounts' central ideas about the Mount Everest disaster. Use the graphic organizer below to help you organize your content.

Title of Your Web Page:
Main Idea of Your Web Page:

Account	Details Emphasized in Account
Method of Organization:	
Connection to Main Idea in *Into Thin Air:*	

SL.9–10.5 | **Write Content** Decide which group members will be responsible for writing each part of the Web page. You will need to write enough to convey your points thoroughly but not so much that readers lose interest. Look at other Web pages and wikis (a wiki page is part of a collection of interlinked pages with a Web browser) online to get ideas about how to break up the text and engage readers.

After all the content is written, peer review each other's work and make sure it all flows together logically and supports the main idea you wanted to convey. Follow the citation guidelines on pages R35–R37 of your textbook to cite your sources.

If you decide that you need to include hyperlinks to other media, you'll need to determine where these links should appear. Use the chart below to compile this information.

Link Needed	Location of Link in Content

Present Your Web Page Content If you are not going on to Part 2 of the 21st Century Skills Project, your teacher may ask you to present your Web page content as the end result of the project. You may also be evaluated on the presentation.

Display your Web page content in a written or typed format that is visually appealing and presents the information clearly. If you have plans to include hyperlinks, indicate where these would appear by underlining the relevant text to be linked and including footnotes that summarize what each link is about. You could also include sample print-outs of the links and number them to match your footnotes. Once your group is satisfied that the content is presented effectively, turn it in to your teacher.

21st Century Skills Project

PART 2 Build a Web Page

W.9–10.7 After you've finished Part 1 of this project, build a Web page for your content. If your school or class already has a wiki, you may want to add your content as a wiki page. There are also many sites that will allow you to create your own Web page for free. These types of sites often provide templates and are easy to use.

Make sure the information on your page is visually appealing, clearly presented, and easy to navigate. Use headings to introduce topics and break up text. Check to make sure you've included all necessary hyperlinks and that they work.

After you've completed this project, answer the following questions.

1. How well does your Web page convey your main idea about the Mount Everest disaster as portrayed in different mediums?

_____

_____

_____

_____

2. Does the main idea of your Web page relate to the main idea of *Into Thin Air*? Explain your thoughts.

_____

_____

_____

_____

3. Is your Web page easy to navigate? Is information presented clearly? Explain your thoughts.

_____

_____

_____

4. What would you change in the planning, creation, and presentation of this project if you were to do it again?

_____

_____

_____

21st Century Skills Project

Evaluate As you read and view your classmates' work, take notes about the content and effectiveness of their Web pages. Then use your notes to participate in a class discussion about the project.

1. Does the main idea about the Mount Everest disaster make sense? Is it adequately supported? Explain your thoughts.

_____

_____

_____

2. Is the comparison of the different accounts clear? Explain your thoughts.

_____

_____

_____

_____

3. Is the information on the Web page presented clearly and effectively? Explain.

_____

_____

_____

_____

4. What would you add or change on the Web page? Why? Consider the content, navigation, and design.

_____

_____

_____

_____

_____

_____

A New Generation of Americans

John F. Kennedy

Glencoe Literature, pages 378–385

RI.9–10.10

Before starting the lesson, read the following selection and complete the lesson activities in *Glencoe Literature*.

"A New Generation of Americans" (pages 378–385)

In this lesson you will analyze and discuss President John F. Kennedy's speech "A New Generation of Americans." You will then plan and create a multimedia exhibit exploring the political and social climate of the United States during the early 1960s. Through your participation in the discussion and your work on the project, you will practice the following standards:

RI.9–10.6

Craft and Structure

- Determine an author's purpose in a text and analyze how an author uses rhetoric to advance that purpose.

**RI.9–10.7
RI.9–10.8
RI.9–10.9**

Integration of Knowledge and Ideas

- Analyze accounts of a subject told in different mediums.
- Evaluate the argument and claims in a text, assessing whether the reasoning is valid and the evidence is relevant and sufficient.
- Identify false statements and fallacious reasoning.
- Analyze U.S. documents of historical and literary significance.

Group Discussion

Discussing a speech, such as "A New Generation of Americans," within a small group can help you grow as a reader and as a member of a learning community. Together, you and other group members can arrive at a better understanding of a selection, its ideas and craft, and its connection to other works and areas of study.

PLAN

**RI.9–10.1
W.9–10.9
W.9–10.9b
W.9–10.10
L.9–10.1
L.9–10.2
L.9–10.2c**

To prepare for discussion, build your content knowledge by examining the selection in greater detail. On your own, write your answers to the questions that follow using text evidence. You may also write additional questions about the selection that you wish to discuss with your group. Your teacher may review your answers before the discussion, so be sure to use correct grammar, spelling, punctuation, and capitalization.

RI.9–10.6 | **Author's Purpose** An author's intent in writing a work is called an **author's purpose**. Authors typically write for one or more of the following purposes: to persuade, to inform, to explain, to entertain, or to describe.

1. Political leaders often make speeches to convince an audience to find common ground and agree on a shared goal. What was President John F. Kennedy's primary purpose in writing his inaugural address "A New Generation of Americans"? Cite words and phrases from the text that make his purpose clear.

_____

_____

_____

_____

RI.9–10.8 | **Argument** An **argument** is a type of persuasive writing in which logic and reason are used to try to influence a reader's ideas or actions. In an argument, a statement of opinion about a problem or an issue is often called a **claim.** The support for a claim includes reasons and evidence. **Reasons** explain why someone should accept the claim. **Evidence** consists of examples, facts, and expert opinions.

2. What is President Kennedy's central claim in the speech? What reasons and evidence does he use to support his claim? Are these reasons and evidence valid, relevant, and sufficient? Explain your answers in the chart below.

Central Claim:		
Reason/Evidence:	Reason/Evidence:	Reason/Evidence:
Validity:	Validity:	Validity:

Group Discussion

RI.9–10.6

Rhetoric Sometimes authors employ **rhetoric**, or the art of using language, to present facts and ideas in order to persuade their readers. **Rhetorical devices** are techniques that writers use to persuade, including repetition, parallelism, antithesis, logic, rhetorical questions, and the skillful use of connotation and anecdote. (See the Literary Terms Handbook, pages R1–R19, in your textbook for full definitions of these terms.)

3. Analyze President Kennedy's use of rhetorical devices within his inaugural address. For each rhetorical device listed below, include an example from "A New Generation of Americans" and explain the effect it has on the audience.

Repetition: _____

_____

_____

_____

_____

_____

Parallelism: _____

_____

_____

_____

_____

Antithesis: _____

_____

_____

_____

Rhetorical Question: _____

_____

_____

_____

_____

_____

Group Discussion

RI.9–10.8 | **Fallacious Reasoning** Even if an argument has a logical structure, it may have illogical elements, including false statements and fallacious reasoning. Examples of false statements and fallacious reasoning include logical and rhetorical fallacies. A **logical fallacy** is an error in reasoning in which the writer tries to make an appeal to logic, but the logic is faulty. A **rhetorical fallacy** is an error in reasoning that occurs when the writer uses misleading appeals to emotions, ethics, or authority.

4. Does the speech contain any examples of false statements or fallacious reasoning? Explain your thoughts.

_____

_____

_____

_____

_____

RI.9–10.7 | **Accounts Across Mediums** Accounts of a subject, such as President Kennedy's "A New Generation of Americans," may be found in different **mediums,** or modes of expression, such as audio recordings, video clips, newspapers, Web sites, or documentaries. When you compare accounts of a subject across different mediums, you determine which details are emphasized in each account. This helps you deepen your understanding of the subject at hand. It also helps you appreciate the particular advantages of each mode of expression.

5. Find an audio or a video recording of President Kennedy's inaugural address either online or on audio or video tapes. Compare the print version of the speech (pages 380–382) with the audio or video recording you've found. What words and phrases are emphasized in each account? Explain how listening to the recording or viewing the video helps you better understand the speech.

_____

_____

_____

_____

_____

_____

RI.9–10.9 **Comparing Texts** Presented to the nation on January 20, 1961, President Kennedy's "A New Generation of Americans" is one of several famous speeches of the era. Another is "I Have a Dream," delivered by Martin Luther King Jr. on August 28, 1963, during the March on Washington for Jobs and Freedom. Many literary and history scholars believe these two public addresses are among the most eloquent and relevant speeches in all of U.S. history.

6. Find King's "I Have a Dream" either online or in a printed book. Read it and compare its content with that of Kennedy's "A New Generation of Americans." Use the chart below to note similarities and differences between the speeches on topics that are common to both. An example has been filled in for you.

Topic	"A New Generation of Americans"	"I Have a Dream"
The Origins of the U.S.	Kennedy reminds Americans that they are "heirs of that first revolution." He believes they should aim to help people in other nations whose human rights may be at risk.	King reminds the public that "every American was to fall heir" to the promises of the Constitution and Declaration of Independence. He argues that the human rights of African Americans have not been honored.
Health of the U.S.		
Threats to the Health of the U.S.		
Freedom and Democracy		
Activism of Americans		

Group Discussion

7. On the basis of these two speeches, what can you conclude about the problems affecting the U.S. during the early 1960s?

_____

_____

_____

_____

_____

_____

_____

_____

_____

_____

8. What similarities and differences do you see in the solutions Kennedy and King propose in their speeches?

_____

_____

_____

_____

_____

_____

_____

_____

_____

_____

_____

ASSIGN

RI.9–10.6
RI.9–10.7
RI.9–10.8
RI.9–10.9
SL.9–10.1
SL.9–10.1a

Meet with your literature group to plan your discussion. Each group member should become the expert on one or more of the questions answered on the previous pages. Each expert will then guide the discussion on his or her question(s). List each group member and the question he or she will become an expert on in the chart below.

Group Member	Question(s) to Present

To become an expert on your question(s), spend some extra time thinking about your questions(s) and consulting the text for relevant details. Building on your question(s), write down one or two discussion points or related questions for group members to consider as they explore text issues.

_____

_____

_____

_____

_____

_____

Group Discussion

DISCUSS

SL.9–10.1
SL.9–10.1a
SL.9–10.1b
SL.9–10.1c
SL.9–10.1d
Break into your assigned literature group to conduct your discussion. The expert for question 1 should begin by reading aloud the question and leading the discussion in response. Follow this process for each question until you have covered them all.

Remember that literature groups contain room for disagreement. Healthy debate can help all members push their understanding to a new level. Use your time wisely so that you are able to discuss all the questions sufficiently.

In your discussion, follow the guidelines below.

Discussion Guidelines

- Come to discussions prepared; be sure you have carefully and thoroughly answered all questions.

- Express your ideas clearly. When presenting on your question and commenting on others, support your ideas with concrete evidence from the text. Give specific page numbers.

- Work with your group to set rules for discussion and decision making (*e.g.,* informal consensus, taking votes on key issues, presenting alternative views).

- Work with your group to set clear goals and deadlines.

- Create individual roles as needed (*e.g.,* note taker, moderator, etc.).

- Propel conversations by posing and responding to questions that relate the current discussion to broader themes or larger ideas (*e.g.,* fantasy versus reality).

- Actively incorporate others into the discussion; clarify, verify, or challenge ideas and conclusions.

- Respond thoughtfully to diverse perspectives and summarize points of agreement and disagreement.

- Qualify or justify your views and understanding and make new connections in light of the evidence and reasoning presented.

At the end of your discussion, be prepared to share the insights you have gained with your class. On the lines below, briefly summarize the most interesting ideas or insights you heard or experienced during the discussion.

_____

_____

_____

_____

_____

A New Generation of Americans
John F. Kennedy

21st Century Skills Project | Multimedia Exhibit

Now that you have analyzed and discussed "A New Generation of Americans" in detail, you will have the opportunity to extend your thinking about it creatively by completing a group project. Your assignment is to develop a proposal for a multimedia exhibit that explores the political and social climate of the United States during the early 1960s. In carrying out this project, you will follow the steps below:

- Conduct research about certain aspects of American culture.
- Organize and write content for a multimedia exhibit proposal.
- If resources allow, you can create and present your multimedia exhibit.

PART 1 Develop a Proposal

With a small group, conduct research into various aspects of American culture in the time of Kennedy and King. Using the information you gather, develop a written proposal for a multimedia exhibit.

RI.9–10.9
SL.9–10.2
W.9–10.7

Conduct Research Using reliable print and online resources, find information about the important political and social issues of the Kennedy-King era. Locate facts in diverse media or formats, such as print sources (books, newspapers, magazines), Web sites, photographs, TV news accounts, and/or documentaries. You might consider consulting the Web sites of the Library of Congress and the John F. Kennedy Presidential Library and Museum during your search. Remember to evaluate the credibility and accuracy of each source. To help you get started, research aspects of American culture that are reflected in "A New Generation of Americans" and "I Have a Dream" and compile your notes in the chart on the next page.

You might wish to address some or all of the following topics:

- John F. Kennedy
- The threat of nuclear destruction
- The Cold War
- U.S. fear of Communism and its global influence
- U.S. assistance to developing nations
- U.S. support of the United Nations (U.N.)
- Martin Luther King Jr.
- Racial segregation and discrimination in the U.S.
- The Civil Rights Movement
- The threat of civil war in the U.S.
- Freedom/Democracy
- Activism of U.S. citizens

21st Century Skills Project

After you've completed the chart, answer the questions that follow to help focus your research.

Aspect of American Culture	Notes
The Cold War	

1. How did your research help you understand the information presented in "A New Generation of Americans" and "I Have a Dream"?

_____

_____

_____

_____

_____

_____

_____

_____

21st Century Skills Project

2. Which aspects of American culture do you want to highlight in your multimedia exhibit? Why?

_____

_____

_____

_____

_____

_____

_____

_____

3 What main idea do you want to convey about the American culture of the Kennedy-King era?

_____

_____

_____

_____

_____

_____

_____

RI.9–10.9 **Organize Information** After you've finished conducting research, you'll need to organize the information that will go in your exhibit proposal with your group. Identify which aspects of American culture you'll focus on in your proposal; what kinds of images, video, sound, or other media you'll include; and how these media will be arranged. As you plan your exhibit, it might help you to think of any museum exhibits you've seen. How were the images and artifacts arranged? By type? Chronologically? In some other way? Finally, think about how the information you've gathered helps you understand the cultural experience of 1960s-era Americans. Use the graphic organizer on the next page to help you organize your content.

21st Century Skills Project

Title of Exhibit:

Main Idea of Exhibit:

Aspect of American Culture	Supporting Media

Method of Media Organization:

Connection to "A New Generation of Americans"/ "I Have a Dream":

Write Proposal Decide which group members will be responsible for writing each part of the proposal. Using the chart you filled out above as a guide, begin by explaining what the title and main idea of your exhibit will be. Then summarize the aspects of American culture you will focus on, the important points you want to make about these aspects, and which media you will use to support your points. Explain how the information in your exhibit will be organized.

After all the content is written, peer review each other's work and make sure it all flows together logically and supports the main idea you want to convey. Follow the citation guidelines on pages R35–R37 of your textbook to cite your sources.

Present Your Proposal If you are not going on to Part 2 of the 21st Century Skills Project, your teacher may ask you to present your proposal as the end result of the project. You may also be evaluated on the presentation.

Display your proposal in a written or typed format that is visually appealing and presents the information clearly. Include sample print-outs of the media you describe in your proposal. Once your group is satisfied that the content is presented effectively, turn it in to your teacher.

21st Century Skills Project

PART 2 Create a Multimedia Exhibit

SL.9–10.5 After you've finished Part 1 of this project, create your multimedia exhibit based on your proposal. With your group, decide how you will present your exhibit.

Make sure the information in your exhibit is visually appealing, clearly presented, and flows together logically. Be sure to make strategic use of digital media to enhance understanding of your findings.

After you've completed this project, answer the following questions.

1. How well does your exhibit convey your main idea about the American culture of the Kennedy-King era?

_____

_____

_____

2. Does your exhibit help explain the political and social issues described in "A New Generation of Americans" and "I Have a Dream"? Explain.

_____

_____

_____

3. Does your exhibit flow well? Is information presented clearly? Explain.

_____

_____

_____

_____

4. What would you change in the planning, creation, and presentation of this project if you were to do it again?

_____

_____

_____

_____

21ˢᵗ Century Skills Project

Evaluate As you read and view your classmates' work, take notes about the content and effectiveness of their multimedia exhibits. Then use your notes to participate in a class discussion about the project.

1. Does the main idea about American culture make sense? Is it adequately supported? Explain your thoughts.

_____

_____

_____

_____

2. Does the exhibit help explain the political and social issues described in "A New Generation of Americans" and "I Have a Dream"? Explain.

_____

_____

_____

_____

3. Is the information in the exhibit presented clearly and effectively? Explain.

_____

_____

_____

_____

4. What would you add or change in the exhibit? Why?

_____

_____

_____

_____

21st Century Skills Project

Put Down the Backpack

Anna Quindlen

Glencoe Literature, pages 412–421

RI.9–10.10

Before starting the lesson, read the following selection and complete the lesson activities in *Glencoe Literature.*

"Put Down the Backpack" (pages 412–421)

In this lesson you will analyze and discuss Anna Quindlen's commencement address "Put Down the Backpack." You will then write your own persuasive speech about an important lesson you've learned. Through your participation in the discussion and your work on the project, you will practice the following standards:

RI.9–10.6

Craft and Structure

- Determine an author's purpose in a text and analyze how an author uses rhetoric to advance that purpose.

RI.9–10.8

Integration of Knowledge and Ideas

- Evaluate the argument and claims in a text, assessing whether the reasoning is valid and the evidence is relevant and sufficient.
- Identify false statements and fallacious reasoning.

Group Discussion

Discussing a persuasive speech, such as "Put Down the Backpack," within a small group can help you grow as a reader and as a member of a learning community. Together, you and other group members can arrive at a better understanding of a selection, its ideas and craft, and its connection to other works and areas of study.

PLAN

RI.9–10.1
W.9–10.9
W.9–10.9b
W.9–10.10
L.9–10.1
L.9–10.2
L.9–10.2c

To prepare for discussion, build your content knowledge by examining the selection in greater detail. On your own, write your answers to the questions that follow using text evidence. You may also write additional questions about the selection that you wish to discuss with your group. Your teacher may review your answers before the discussion, so be sure to use correct grammar, spelling, punctuation, and capitalization.

Group Discussion

Group Discussion

RI.9–10.6 | **Author's Purpose** An author's intent in writing a work is called an **author's purpose**. Authors typically write for one or more of the following purposes: to persuade, to inform, to explain, to entertain, or to describe.

1. As you learned in your textbook, Anna Quindlen's primary purpose in writing "Put Down the Backpack" is to persuade her audience to behave in a certain way. Identify the action that Quindlen would like her audience to take. What words and phrases in the speech make her purpose clear?

_____

_____

_____

_____

_____

_____

_____

_____

_____

2. Often a writer has more than one purpose for writing. What other purpose does Quindlen seem to have in writing her commencement address? Cite evidence from the selection to support your answer.

_____

_____

_____

_____

_____

_____

_____

_____

RI.9–10.8 | **Argument** An **argument** is a type of persuasive writing in which logic and reason are used to try to influence a reader's ideas or actions. In an argument, a statement of opinion about a problem or an issue is often called a **claim.** The support for a claim includes reasons and evidence. **Reasons** explain why someone should accept the claim. **Evidence** consists of examples, facts, and expert opinions.

3. What is Quindlen's central claim in the speech? What reasons and evidence does she use to support this claim? Are these reasons and evidence valid, relevant, and sufficient? Explain your answers in the chart below.

Central Claim:		
Reason/Evidence:	**Reason/Evidence:**	**Reason/Evidence:**
Validity:	**Validity:**	**Validity:**

Group Discussion

RI.9–10.6 **Rhetoric** Speech writers often employ **rhetoric,** or the art of using language, to present facts and ideas in order to persuade their readers. **Rhetorical devices** are techniques that writers use to persuade, including repetition, parallelism, analogy, logic, rhetorical questions, and the skillful use of connotation and anecdote. (See the Literary Terms Handbook, pages R1–R19, in your textbook for full definitions of these terms.)

4. Identify an example of logic and an example of anecdote in the speech. How do these rhetorical devices support Quindlen's purpose to persuade her audience?

_____

_____

_____

_____

_____

_____

_____

_____

RI.9–10.8 **Fallacious Reasoning** Even if an argument has a logical structure, it may have illogical elements, including false statements and fallacious reasoning. Examples of false statements and fallacious reasoning include logical and rhetorical fallacies. A **logical fallacy** is an error in reasoning in which the writer tries to make an appeal to logic, but the logic is faulty. A **rhetorical fallacy** is an error in reasoning that occurs when the writer uses misleading appeals to emotions, ethics, or authority.

5. Does the speech contain any examples of false statements or fallacious reasoning? Explain your thoughts.

_____

_____

_____

_____

_____

_____

_____

Group Discussion

ASSIGN

RI.9–10.6
RI.9–10.8
SL.9–10.1
SL.9–10.1a

Meet with your literature group to plan your discussion. Each group member should become the expert on one or more of the questions answered on the previous pages. Each expert will then guide the discussion on his or her question(s). List each group member and the question he or she will become an expert on in the chart below.

Group Member	Question(s) to Present

To become an expert on your question(s), spend some extra time thinking about your question(s) and consulting the text for relevant details. Building on your question(s), write down one or two discussion points or related questions for group members to consider as they explore text issues.

_____

_____

_____

_____

_____

Group Discussion

DISCUSS

SL.9–10.1a
SL.9–10.1b
SL.9–10.1c
SL.9–10.1d
Break into your assigned literature group to conduct your discussion. The expert for question 1 should begin by reading aloud the question and leading the discussion in response. Follow this process for each question until you have covered them all.

Remember that literature groups contain room for disagreement. Healthy debate can help all members push their understanding to a new level. Use your time wisely so that you are able to discuss all the questions sufficiently.

In your discussion, follow the guidelines below.

Discussion Guidelines

- Come to discussions prepared; be sure you have carefully and thoroughly answered all questions.
- Express your ideas clearly. When presenting on your question and commenting on others, support your ideas with concrete evidence from the text. Give specific page numbers.
- Work with your group to set rules for discussion and decision making (*e.g.,* informal consensus, taking votes on key issues, presenting alternative views).
- Work with your group to set clear goals and deadlines.
- Create individual roles as needed (*e.g.,* note taker, moderator, etc.).
- Propel conversations by posing and responding to questions that relate the current discussion to broader themes or larger ideas (*e.g.,* fantasy versus reality).
- Actively incorporate others into the discussion; clarify, verify, or challenge ideas and conclusions.
- Respond thoughtfully to diverse perspectives and summarize points of agreement and disagreement.
- Qualify or justify your views and understanding and make new connections in light of the evidence and reasoning presented.

At the end of your discussion, be prepared to share the insights you have gained with your class. On the lines below, briefly summarize the most interesting ideas or insights you heard or experienced during the discussion.

_____

_____

_____

_____

_____

_____

Put Down the Backpack
Anna Quindlen

21st Century Skills Project Multimedia Speech

Now that you have analyzed and discussed "Put Down the Backpack" in detail, you will have the opportunity to extend your thinking about it creatively by completing a project. Your assignment is to write a persuasive speech in which you advise younger siblings, friends, and/or classmates to learn from your past experiences and take a particular course of action. In carrying out this project, you will follow the steps below:

- Conduct research on the topic you will be discussing.
- Organize, write content for, and orally present your speech.
- If resources allow, you can publish your speech online.

PART 1 Write a Persuasive Speech

Anna Quindlen delivered her speech at the graduation ceremonies of Mount Holyoke College, in South Hadley, Massachusetts, on May 23, 1999, imparting information that she thought would be helpful to the new graduates as they entered "the real world." Write your own persuasive speech in which you share a valuable lesson that you've learned and try to convince others to adopt your position and/or take an action.

Plan Your Speech First, choose a lesson that has left a strong impression on you and that you can develop more fully through research. Remember that you will be presenting your speech to the class; consult with your teacher to make sure that your topic is appropriate. Here are some topics you might consider:

- being a good friend
- setting and achieving a personal goal
- being true to yourself
- helping others/volunteering
- taking care of the environment
- participating in a favorite sport or activity
- overcoming a disappointment or failure
- keeping an open mind about new people or situations
- having enough "free" time
- being healthy
- avoiding technology overload

21st Century Skills Project

Next, clearly formulate your claim—your position on the topic you've chosen. Then find specific reasoning and evidence, such as facts and studies, which support your position. Anticipate objections that others might have to your ideas; acknowledge the objections and convincingly demonstrate that your position is the correct one. Sequence your reasons and evidence so that your speech will have a smooth progression of ideas.

SL.9–10.2
W.9–10.7

Conduct Research Conduct research on the life lesson you are addressing. Using reliable print and online sources, find information about your topic that will help support your argument. Look for facts (such as statistics), studies, anecdotes, and expert testimony that will make your position stronger or easier to understand. For example, you might locate anecdotes from successful individuals about the value of overcoming failure or scientific studies about the importance of eating well. Take notes as you research to help you write the points of your speech.

Organize Content After you've completed your research, you will need to organize the content of your speech. Come up with three or four main reasons for your position. The reasons should flow together logically and be supported by strong evidence. Organize the relevant research notes for each reason. Depending on your teacher's guidelines, you will likely have only five to six minutes to present your speech, so you will need to emphasize only the most important points. Set aside any notes that are irrelevant or unimportant.

Use the following outline to help you organize your points.

Speech Topic:_____

Claim/Position: _____

  I. Reason:_____

    A. _____

    B. _____

  II. Reason:_____

    A. _____

    B. _____

  III. Reason:_____

    A. _____

    B. _____

  IV. Reason:_____

    A. _____

    B. _____

W.9–10.1
W.9–10.1a
W.9–10.1b
W.9–10.1c
W.9–10.1d
W.9–10.1e

Write Speech After you've finished organizing your content, you'll need to write your speech. Keep the following tips in mind:

- Introduce your claim, or position, with a provocative question or humorous comment to engage your listeners' attention.
- Present your points as you outlined them, being sure to support each point with strong evidence, such as relevant personal anecdotes or facts.
- Use transitional words and phrases to link sections of text.
- Use rhetorical devices, such as repetition, parallelism, analogy, logic, rhetorical questions, and the skillful use of connotation and anecdote. (See the Literary Terms Handbook, pages R1–R19, in your textbook for term definitions.)
- Address possible objections to your argument with strong reasons why your position is correct.
- Avoid fallacious reasoning or exaggerated or distorted evidence.
- Provide a conclusion that logically follows from your argument.
  After all the content for the speech is written, have a peer review your work to make sure it all flows together logically and forms a coherent argument.

SL.9–10.4
SL.9–10.6

Present Your Speech Now that you have written the content of your speech, present it to your class. Keep the following tips in mind:

- Speak clearly and maintain eye contact with your audience.
- Vary your intonation to draw attention to your points.
- Adapt your speech to the context and demonstrate a command of formal English.
- Present your points and supporting evidence clearly, concisely, and logically.
- Be sure that the organization, development, and content of your argument are appropriate to the purpose, audience, and task.
- Use rhetoric to support your points.
- Avoid fallacious reasoning or exaggerated or distorted evidence.

RI.9–10.8
SL.9–10.3

When it is your classmates' turn to present, be sure to listen to others' speeches attentively. Use the following questions to help you evaluate other speakers' points:

- Is the speaker's position clear? Are the speaker's points clear, and are they supported by evidence and rhetoric?
- Are the speaker's points logical? Can you follow his or her line of reasoning?
- Does the speaker adequately address possible objections to his or her argument?
- Does the speaker include any fallacious reasoning or exaggerated or distorted evidence? Explain.

If you are not going on to Part 2 of the 21st Century Skills Project, your teacher may ask you to present your written speech as the end result of the project after you have given it orally. Present your speech in a written or typed format that is neat and clearly organized. You may wish to incorporate feedback from classmates in order to strengthen your speech. Make sure each point is addressed and supported with evidence. Once you are satisfied that its content is presented effectively, turn it in to your teacher.

21st Century Skills Project

PART 2 Publish Online

SL.9–10.5 After you've finished Part 1 of this project, publish your speech online in an interactive format that includes an audio recording of your speech and hyperlinks to articles, images, and other visual media, such as video clips. Make strategic use of digital media to enhance understanding of your speech. If you wish to change some of your content or add to it based on what you learned during your presentation of Part 1 of the 21st Century Skills Project, you may do so.

SL.9–10.6 **Audio Recording** Before you record your speech, practice reading it aloud. Don't rush as you read. Use your punctuation and line breaks to determine where to pause. Be sure to adapt your speech to the context. For example, if your speech is written using relatively formal language, don't read it with an informal tone of voice. When you feel prepared, record your speech.

Links to Media When you publish your speech, you will include hyperlinks to media, which will elaborate on the evidence, images, and other details you've included in your speech. These links will help your readers get a better understanding of your topic, your position, your reasons, and your evidence. For example, if your speech argued the value of performing in a musical band, you might choose to include links to relevant testimonials from professional musicians as well as video clips and/or audio clips of one of your performances. Your links should relate to your topic and boost the persuasiveness of your speech. Pay attention to copyright information when you choose your media. Include credit information if you need to.

Before you publish your speech, fill in the chart below to help you decide what images and other media you want to include.

Idea in Speech	Location (paragraph and line)	Corresponding Media Link

W.9–10.6 **Publish and Present** After you've completed your chart, decide where you will publish your speech. If your school already has a Web site for students, you might consider publishing your speech there. You can also search online for Web sites that allow you to create your own page for free. These types of sites often provide templates and are easy to use.

Publish your speech on your chosen site. Using your chart as a guide, hyperlink various ideas or images in your speech to photos and other media. Add a hyperlink to your audio recording at the beginning of the speech. When you're finished, send the URL of your site to your teacher and classmates so they can read and view your work.

After you've completed this project, answer the following questions.

1. How well does the content of your online speech, including your recording of the speech and the hyperlinks you included, convey your argument? Explain your thoughts.

_____

_____

_____

_____

_____

_____

2. Which ideas or images in your speech led to the most interesting links? Why?

_____

_____

_____

_____

3. What would you change in the planning, creation, and presentation of this project if you were to do it again?

_____

_____

_____

_____

21st Century Skills Project

RI.9–10.8 **Evaluate** As you read and view your classmates' work, take notes about the content and effectiveness of their multimedia speeches. Then use your notes to participate in a class discussion about the project.

1. Does the multimedia version of the speech convey the argument effectively? Explain your thoughts.

_____
_____
_____
_____
_____

2. Does the audio recording add to or detract from your understanding of the speech? Explain your thoughts.

_____
_____
_____
_____

3. How well do the links connect to ideas and images in the speech? Explain.

_____
_____
_____
_____

4. What would you add or change in the speech or the accompanying media? Why?

_____
_____
_____
_____

21st Century Skills Project

Writing Workshops

Writing Workshop
PERSUASIVE SPEECH

Glencoe Literature Connection: The Gettysburg Address, page 376

Before starting the lesson, read the following selection in **Glencoe Literature**.

The Gettysburg Address by Abraham Lincoln **(page 376)**

In this lesson, you will study Abraham Lincoln's Gettysburg Address to discover how the author effectively uses the argumentative writing methods and techniques listed below. You will then write your own persuasive speech using these methods and techniques. As you complete this workshop, you will practice the following standards:

W.9–10.1, a
W.9–10.1, b

Develop Claims and Counterclaims

- Introduce claims.
- Distinguish claims from alternate or opposing claims.
- Create an organization that establishes clear relationships among claims, counterclaims, reasons, and evidence.
- Provide evidence for claims and counterclaims while pointing out the strengths and limitations of both in a way that anticipates the audience's concerns.

W.9–10.1, c

Use Transitions and Parallelism

- Use words, phrases, and clauses to link sections of text.
- Use transitions and parallelism to create cohesion and clarify the relationships between claims, counterclaims, reasons, and evidence.

W.9–10.1, d

Establish and Maintain an Appropriate Style and Tone

- Establish and maintain a formal style and an objective tone.
- Use the norms and conventions of persuasive writing and speaking.

W.9–10.1, e

Provide a Conclusion

- Provide a conclusion that follows from and supports the argument presented.

Argument

Analyze and Prewrite

Develop Claims and Counterclaims

Persuasion is writing that attempts to convince readers to think or act in a certain way. An **argument** is a type of persuasive writing in which logic and reason are used to try to influence a reader's thoughts or actions. In an argument, a statement of opinion about a problem or an issue is often called a **claim**. The support for a claim includes reasons and evidence. **Reasons** explain why someone should accept the claim. **Evidence** consists of examples, facts, and opinions. In addition, arguments often include **counterclaims,** or brief arguments that attempt to disprove opposing opinions about the problem or issue.

LEARN FROM THE MODEL

Skim the Gettysburg Address again to see how President Lincoln develops his argument. Notice that in the speech, the claim of his opponents is implied rather than directly stated. In general, President's Lincoln's opponents were supporters of the Confederate cause.

1. Use the chart below to explore the central claim, opposing claim, and counterclaim that President Lincoln presents or suggests in his speech.

Stated Central Claim:	
Implied Opposing Claim:	
Stated Counterclaim:	
Support for Claim and/or Counterclaim:	**Support for Claim and/or Counterclaim:**

Argument

2. Why do you suppose President Lincoln implies but does not state the claim of his opponents in his speech?

_____

_____

_____

W.9–10.1, a
W.9–10.1, b

APPLY WHAT YOU'VE LEARNED

3. What topic will your persuasive speech be about? What claim(s) do you want to make about this topic?

_____

_____

_____

4. What reasons, evidence, and counterclaims will you use to support your claim? Use the outline below to create an organization that establishes clear relationships among claims, counterclaims, reasons, and evidence.

Speech Topic: _____

Claim: _____

    I. _____

      A. _____

      B. _____

    II. _____

      A. _____

      B. _____

    III. _____

      A. _____

      B. _____

Argument

Use Transitions and Parallelism

Skilled speech writers often rely on two devices to link sections of text and create a cohesive, or organized, argument: transitions and parallelism. A **transition** is a connecting word, phrase, or clause that clarifies relationships between details, sentences, or paragraphs. Some common transitional words and phrases include *first, next, after, in a similar way, above all, then,* and *finally.* **Parallelism** is the use of a series of words, phrases, or sentences that have similar grammatical form. John F. Kennedy's "A New Generation of Americans" (pages 378–385) contains this famous example of parallelism: "Let every nation know, whether it wishes us well or ill, that we shall pay any price, bear any burden, meet any hardship, support any friend, oppose any foe to assure the survival and success of liberty."

LEARN FROM THE MODEL

Reread passages from the Gettysburg Address as indicated below and analyze President Lincoln's use of transitions and parallelism.

1. Identify the transitional word or phrase that President Lincoln uses in the second sentence of the speech. What shift does this transition signal?

_____

_____

_____

_____

2. Review the first sentence of the second paragraph of the speech. Identify the transitional word or phrase within the passage. Is this transition effective? Why or why not?

_____

_____

_____

_____

_____

_____

_____

Argument

3. Identify at least three examples of parallelism within the speech. Explain how each example helps to clarify relationships between ideas and create a cohesive, or organized, argument.

Parallelism	How It Helps Clarify Ideas

W.9–10.1, c **APPLY WHAT YOU'VE LEARNED**

4. Review your outline on page 141. What words, phrases, or clauses would help make your transitions from point to point clear? Jot down several possible transitions below.

_____

_____

_____

_____

_____

5. Pick one claim from your outline and write a few sentences using parallelism to link this claim to its supporting evidence.

_____

_____

_____

_____

_____

_____

_____

Argument

Establish and Maintain an Appropriate Style and Tone

In an argument, it is important for writers to maintain a relatively formal style and an objective tone, or attitude, so that readers think the argument is credible. For example, if a writer presented an argument in favor of a later starting time for his or her high school and included a statement such as "I think school should start later because I'm really tired every morning," the reader would not be likely to take the writer seriously. The tone of the statement is subjective (about the writer's personal experiences) and is presented casually. The writer would sound more credible if he or she presented an objective reason for a later starting time and used a more formal style. A statement such as, "Studies have shown that students benefit from a later start time" would probably be more effective.

LEARN FROM THE MODEL

Reread passages from the Gettysburg Address as indicated below and analyze the style and tone President Lincoln establishes and maintains throughout his speech.

1. Review the first paragraph of the speech. What words and phrases contribute to a formal style? How? Find at least three examples. Use the chart below to address these questions.

Word or Phrase	How It Contributes to Formal Style

2. How would you describe the tone, or attitude, of President Lincoln's Gettysburg Address? Support your response with evidence from the text.

_____

_____

_____

_____

_____

APPLY WHAT YOU'VE LEARNED

3. Look at your outline on page 141 and choose one paragraph to develop on the lines below. Focus on establishing and maintaining a formal style and an objective tone as you write.

_____

_____

_____

_____

_____

_____

_____

_____

_____

_____

Provide a Conclusion

An effective conclusion in an argument should follow from and support the argument that the writer is making. Strong conclusions often include a call to action or a comment that gives the reader something additional to consider.

LEARN FROM THE MODEL

Reread passages from the Gettysburg Address as indicated below and analyze the effectiveness of speech's conclusion.

1. Reread the last sentence of the speech. What call to action does President Lincoln include here? How does it relate to the rest of his argument?

_____

_____

_____

_____

_____

_____

_____

2. With what final thought does President Lincoln end his speech? Is this an effective concluding statement? Why or why not?

_____

_____

_____

_____

_____

_____

_____

W.9–10.1, e | **APPLY WHAT YOU'VE LEARNED**

3. Use the lines below to jot down possible ideas for the conclusion of your speech. What call to action or additional thought will you include? How will the conclusion relate to the rest of your speech?

_____

_____

_____

_____

_____

_____

_____

_____

_____

_____

_____

_____

_____

_____

Argument

Draft

W.9–10.10
Before you begin drafting, review your prewriting notes on pages 140–146. Then write your first draft on a computer, following the instructions below.

Write the Introduction

W.9–10.1, d
Begin by writing the introductory paragraph or paragraphs of your persuasive speech. Your introduction should include

- a statement of your position on the issue and your basic reason for holding it
- a statement of what you want your reader to do in response
- an explanation of the context of your argument (or at least a reference to the context if you can assume your reader knows about it)
- an explanation of why your topic matters

Remember to establish a formal style and an objective tone in your introduction.

Write the Body

W.9–10.1, a
W.9–10.1, b
W.9–10.1, c
W.9–10.1, d
Use your outline to guide you as you write the body of your speech. Remember to support your claims with reasons and evidence. You will also need to distinguish your claims from alternate or opposing claims and include counterclaims, or brief arguments that attempt to disprove opposing opinions. One way to do this is to use transitional words, phrases or clauses to create cohesion, or clarity, between the different claims. You might wish to present claims, opposing claims, and counterclaims by using sentence frames like the following:

- "Opponents to this issue say that _____, but the evidence shows that _____."

- "Many will probably disagree with my assertion that _____, because _____, but _____."

- "Some of you may challenge my claim that _____. After all, many believe that _____. Indeed, my own claim that _____ seems to ignore _____. However, _____."

Be sure to develop your claims and counterclaims fairly by supplying evidence to support them. Point out the strengths and limitations of your claims and counterclaims based on your audience's knowledge level and concerns. Read the annotated model on the next page to get an idea of how to present claims, opposing views, counterclaims, and evidence.

Claim: The starting time for our school should be changed from 7:00 A.M. to 8:00 A.M. to give students extra time for sleep.

Opposing View: Opponents of the later starting time have blamed students' sleep habits, rather than the school's schedule, for the fact that students are so sleepy. Several community members have argued that we should focus on teaching students to go to bed earlier.

Counterclaim and Evidence: While it is true that students need to be taught good sleep habits, studies have shown that teenagers actually remain more alert later at night than adults. In addition, they continue producing melatonin, the chemical responsible for sleepiness, far longer into the morning than adults.

Anticipation of Audience Concern: Changing the starting time for school would enable students to live healthier lives and do better academically, things we all care about.

Argument

Note that the writer anticipates possible concerns from the audience about the later starting time by acknowledging the validity of the opposing claim ("While it is true that students need to be taught good sleep habits"). The writer then presents a solid counterclaim that is supported by evidence. The writer proceeds to anticipate further audience concerns about students' health by stating that the later starting time would improve students' health.

As you write, make sure the organization of your speech establishes clear relationships among claims, counterclaims, reasons, and evidence. Maintain the formal style and objective tone that you established in the introduction.

Write the Conclusion

W.9–10.1, e | Finally, write the conclusion of your speech. Make sure it follows from and supports your argument. Your conclusion could be a single paragraph, or it could be several paragraphs, depending on what you want to do in it. Following are some things a well-written conclusion can do:

- restate your main claim forcefully or with an added twist
- summarize your strongest claims
- present a final synthesis of all your ideas
- connect persuasively with your audience
- suggest next steps, questions, or areas of exploration

Revise

W.9–10.4
W.9–10.5

To revise your speech, you will be focusing on the content, or the message, of your writing and possibly applying one or more of these four revision strategies:

- **add** details and information to make the message clearer
- **remove** distracting or unnecessary words or ideas
- **replace** bland or overused language with more precise or stronger words
- **rearrange** phrases and sentences to be sure the message is logically presented

The questions that follow will show you how to use these revision strategies. They will help you consider how well the development, organization, and style of your speech are appropriate to task, purpose, and audience.

Focus and Coherence

Ask yourself the following questions. Then evaluate your speech and check each box when your speech meets the criteria.

☐ Does my speech have a clear focus?

☐ Do all the parts work together so that I achieve my purpose?

Organization

W.9–10.1, a
W.9–10.1, e

Ask yourself the following questions. Then evaluate your speech and check each box when your speech meets the criteria.

☐ Does the beginning introduce my argument and its significance?

☐ Does the middle follow an organization that establishes clear relationships among claims, counterclaims, reasons and evidence?

☐ Does the conclusion follow from and support my argument?

Development of Ideas

W.9–10.1, a
W.9–10.1, b

Ask yourself the following questions. Then evaluate your speech and check each box when your speech meets the criteria.

☐ Did I introduce claims and distinguish them from alternate or opposing claims?

☐ Did I develop my claims and counterclaims fairly, supplying evidence for each?

☐ Did I present the strengths and limitations of my claims and counterclaims in a way that anticipates my audience's knowledge level and concerns?

Argument

Voice—Word Choice

W.9–10.1, d
L.9–10.3

Ask yourself the following questions. Then evaluate your speech and check each box when your speech meets the criteria.

☐ Is my choice of words persuasive?

☐ Did I establish and maintain a formal style and an objective tone?

☐ Did I apply knowledge of language to make effective choices for meaning or style?

Voice—Sentence Fluency

W.9–10.1, c

Ask yourself the following questions. Then evaluate your speech and check each box when your speech meets the criteria.

☐ Does my writing flow smoothly?

☐ Does my speech include transitional words, phrases, and clauses to link major sections of text?

☐ Did I use words, phrases, and clauses to clarify the relationships between claims, counterclaims, reasons, and evidence?

☐ Did I emphasize important points?

Edit and Proofread

Correct Errors in Grammar

L.9–10.3, a

Editing involves correcting errors in grammar, usage, mechanics, and spelling. As you edit, make sure your work conforms to the guidelines in a style manual that is appropriate for this type of writing. Check with your teacher to see which style guide you should use for reference.

Begin the editing stage by taking a careful look at your sentences. Make sure that each sentence expresses a complete thought in a way that is grammatically correct. Use the checklist that follows to edit your sentences.

SENTENCE-EDITING CHECKLIST

☐ Have I avoided sentence fragments?

☐ Have I avoided run-on sentences?

☐ Do verbs agree with their subjects?

☐ Are pronouns used correctly?

☐ Are verbs used correctly?

☐ Have I avoided misplaced and dangling modifiers?

☐ Have I used phrases and clauses correctly?

☐ Have I used parallel structure?

Argument

Correct Errors in Mechanics and Spelling

L.9–10.2, c | Next, check for and correct any errors in mechanics (punctuation and capitalization) and spelling.

Use the checklist below to edit your speech.

You should also use a dictionary to check and confirm spellings.

PROOFREADING CHECKLIST

☐ Are commas and other punctuation marks used as needed?

☐ Are all words spelled correctly?

☐ Are capital letters used as needed?

Present/Publish

W.9–10.6 | After you have written and polished your speech, you will want to publish and present it. You may wish to consider some of these publishing and presenting options:

- Present your speech orally to your class.
- Use your speech as a springboard for a class debate.
- Publish a multimedia version of your speech online with accompanying links and images.

Consider using technology, including the Internet, to publish your speech, taking advantage of technology's capacity to display information flexibly and dynamically. You may wish to consult some of the projects in the Reading section of this book for additional publishing ideas that include technology.

Argument

Grammar Practice

Clauses and Phrases

L.9–10.1, b | Clauses and phrases are the building blocks of writing. They function to communicate, just as words do, but contain two or more—often many more—words.

Clauses

A group of words with a verb and its subject is a **clause**, whether it is an **independent** clause (one that can stand alone as a sentence) or is a **dependent** clause (one that depends on the independent clause for its meaning) within a sentence. There are a number of kinds of dependent clauses. They are named for the way they function in a sentence: noun clauses, adjective clauses (which are sometimes called "relative clauses"), and adverb clauses. In the following examples, dependent clauses are underlined.

Example	Type of Clause
President Lincoln cared about <u>those who had died</u>.	**Noun clause:** dependent clause used as a noun. In this example, the clause is the object of the preposition *about*.
Many of those <u>who heard the speech</u> did not, at the time, realize its importance.	**Adjective clause:** dependent clause that modifies a noun or a pronoun. It usually follows the word it modifies. Adjective clauses may be introduced by the pronouns *who, whose, that,* and *which* and the conjunctions *where* and *when*. In this example, the clause modifies *those*.
<u>When President Lincoln wrote it</u>, he described the idea of what made America unusual.	**Adverb clause:** dependent clause that modifies a verb, an adjective, or an adverb. It tells *when, where, how, why, to what extent,* or *under what condition*. In this example, the clause modifies *described*.

Exercise A: Identifying Kinds of Dependent Clauses

For each sentence below, identify the kind of clause the underlined words form. Then write **n**, **adj**, or **adv** on the line to identify the type of dependent clause it is.

____ **1.** <u>That all men are created equal</u> was a previously unknown concept.

____ **2.** Part of the battlefield was dedicated to the men <u>who died there</u>.

____ **3.** <u>Before I read the speech</u>, I did not know that it was so short.

____ **4.** President Lincoln wanted the people <u>who heard the speech</u> to dedicate themselves to a great task.

____ **5.** This task involved devotion to <u>the cause for which the men fought</u>.

Phrases

A **phrase** is a group of words that does not contain both a verb and its subject. It acts as a single part of speech in a sentence. Phrases can never stand alone. Seven types of phrases will be covered in this lesson.

Noun Phrase A noun phrase is a noun or pronoun with all its modifiers. The entire group of words functions in the sentence as a noun. Therefore, it might be the subject or object of a verb or a predicate nominative. The underlined examples below are all noun phrases.

> <u>The great president Abraham Lincoln</u> wrote <u>a short but famous speech</u> about <u>brave and dedicated soldiers</u> and <u>a nation at war</u>.

Verb Phrase A verb phrase is a main verb with its helping verb or verbs. The underlined examples below are both verb phrases.

> Many people <u>have believed</u> that the speech <u>was written</u> as President Lincoln traveled.

Prepositional Phrase A prepositional phrase is a phrase that begins with a preposition and ends with a noun or pronoun, which is called "the object of the preposition." The underlined examples below are all prepositional phrases.

> I read <u>through the speech</u> and looked <u>at the reasons for its fame</u>.

Adjective Phrase An adjective phrase is a group of words that modifies a noun or pronoun. Adjective phrases are often prepositional phrases functioning as adjectives, such as the one shown above: "for its fame." However, adjective phrases can also be distinct from prepositional phrases, as in the underlined example below.

> Although the speech is <u>quite short</u>, it mentions one of the most important concepts that we embrace.

Argument

Adverb Phrase An adverb phrase is a group of words that functions as an adverb. Like adjective phrases, adverb phrases are often prepositional phrases, such as the one shown on the previous page: "through the speech." Like adjective phrases, adverb phrases can also be distinct from prepositional phrases, as in the underlined example below.

President Lincoln <u>well and completely</u> knew just how much was sacrificed by those who died at Gettysburg.

Participial Phrase A participle is a verb form that can function as an adjective. A participial phrase is a participle (present or past) combined with complements and modifiers to form a phrase. Since participles as verbals always act as adjectives, participial phrases always do too. The underlined words below are both participial phrases.

<u>Reading the speech</u>, I found myself <u>moved by it</u>.

Absolute Phrase Absolute phrases are different from any other type of phrase in that they modify not a word in a sentence but the entire sentence by adding information about it. Absolute phrases always contain a noun or pronoun and a participle, though they may also contain related modifiers. The underlined words in the sentence below are both absolute phrases.

<u>The speech having been written and rewritten</u>, President Lincoln delivered it.

<u>The speech presented</u>, many must have felt moved.

Exercise B: Identifying Phrases

For each sentence below, identify the kind of phrase the underlined words form: noun, verb, prepositional, adjective, adverb, participial, absolute. In some cases, you may need to identify a phrase as two kinds (for example, prepositional and adjective).

6. A famous and brutal battle of the U.S. Civil War <u>was fought</u> in Gettysburg, Pennsylvania.

_____

_____

7. President Lincoln visited the site <u>on November 19, 1863</u>, four and a half months after the battle.

_____

_____

8. The purpose of the president's visit was to dedicate <u>part of the site</u> as a national military cemetery.

_____

9. Edward Everett, <u>among the most famous orators of the time</u>, spoke before the president.

_____

10. <u>Still and subdued</u>, the audience patiently listened to Everett for nearly two hours.

_____

11. President Lincoln delivered the Gettysburg Address <u>after Everett's remarks</u>.

_____

12. <u>Carrying power</u>, the president's high tenor voice could be heard by the farthest listeners.

_____

13. The president <u>was interrupted</u> by applause five times.

_____

14. President Lincoln's speech was <u>well and truly</u> shorter than Everett's, lasting approximately three minutes.

_____

15. <u>The president's personal secretary</u> wrote in his diary: "the President, in a fine, free way, with more grace than is his wont, said his half dozen words of consecration."

_____

Argument

16. The solemn occasion offered citizens an opportunity <u>in which to remember and mourn the Union dead</u>.

_____

17. <u>The war having continued for years</u>, the endurance of the nation was tested.

_____

Check Your Writing

Check your persuasive speech to make sure you have used phrases and clauses correctly. Make sure you have used various types of phrases and dependent clauses to convey specific meanings and to add variety and interest to your speech. Using phrases and dependent clauses will help you avoid a short, choppy style in your writing.

Argument

Writing Workshop
RESEARCH REPORT
Glencoe Literature Connection: Rosie the Riveter:
Everyday Hero, pages 966–969

Before starting the lesson, read the following selection in **Glencoe Literature.**

"Rosie the Riveter: Everyday Hero" (pages 966–969)

In this lesson, you will study the student model "Rosie the Riveter: Everyday Hero" to discover how the author effectively uses the informative/explanatory writing and research methods and techniques listed below. You will then write your own research report using these methods and techniques. As you complete this workshop, you will practice the following standards:

W.9–10.7
W.9–10.8

Conduct Research

- Conduct research to answer a question or solve a problem.
- Gather information from multiple authoritative print and digital sources.
- Assess the usefulness of each source in answering the research question.
- Synthesize multiple sources.
- Integrate information into the text to maintain the flow of ideas.
- Follow a standard format for citations.

W.9–10.2, a
W.9–10.2, b

Develop a Topic

- Introduce and develop a topic.
- Organize complex ideas, concepts, and information.
- Include formatting, graphics, and multimedia.

W.9–10.2, c
W.9–10.2, d

Use Transitions and Precise Language

- Use appropriate and varied transitions.
- Use precise language and domain-specific vocabulary.

W.9–10.2, e

Establish and Maintain an Appropriate Style and Tone

- Establish and maintain a formal style and an objective tone.
- Use the norms and conventions of informative/explanatory texts.

W.9–10.2, f

Provide a Conclusion

- Provide a conclusion that follows from and supports the information or explanation presented.

Informative Text

Analyze and Prewrite

Conduct Research

Informative/explanatory texts, or expository texts, examine and convey complex ideas, concepts and information. One type of informative/explanatory text that you are probably familiar with is a research report. This type of writing involves exploring a topic by conducting original research, evaluating the research of others, or a combination of both. The writer may also state an opinion on a topic and back it up with evidence found in outside sources.

Writers often choose their topics by thinking about their interests and considering what resources are available. A writer should narrow or broaden a research topic based on the resources available. If only one source exists on a topic, a writer will have a hard time gathering enough information about it. On the other hand, if an enormous number of sources are available, it may be difficult for a writer to sort through them all.

Once a writer chooses a topic, he or she often generates one major question about the topic that can be answered in the report. For example, if someone were to write a report about the *Brown* v. *Board of Education* court case, a research question might be, "Why does this court decision matter?"

As writers conduct research on their topics, they gather relevant information from multiple authoritative sources and assess the usefulness of each source in answering the research question. Writers may need to broaden or narrow their inquiry as they proceed, based on information they discover.

LEARN FROM THE MODEL

Skim "Rosie the Riveter: Everyday Hero" again to determine what research methods the author may have used.

1. What is the topic of this report? What major research question might the author have used to help focus the report?

_____

_____

_____

_____

Informative Text

2. Based on the Works Cited list on page 969, does it seem as though the author used multiple authoritative print and digital sources? Which sources do you think were particularly helpful in addressing the research question? Explain your thoughts.

_____

_____

_____

_____

_____

_____

_____

_____

_____

APPLY WHAT YOU'VE LEARNED

W.9–10.7
W.9–10.8

3. What topic will your research report be about? Remember that your topic shouldn't be too narrow (not enough information is available) or too broad (too much information is available).

_____

_____

_____

_____

4. What will your major research question be?

_____

_____

_____

_____

5. What authoritative print and online sources will you use to gather information? List at least five possible sources on the lines below.

_____

_____

_____

_____

_____

Develop a Topic

Skilled writers of informative/explanatory texts choose to write about topics that are interesting and can be developed adequately with well-chosen, relevant, and sufficient facts; extended definitions; concrete details; quotations; and so on.

LEARN FROM THE MODEL

Reexamine the body paragraphs of "Rosie the Riveter: Everyday Hero" to see how the author develops the topic.

1. What facts, details, and other support does the author use to develop the topic throughout the report? Record your answers in the chart below.

Support Used to Develop Topic:	Support Used to Develop Topic:	Support Used to Develop Topic:

Informative Text

2. What organizational structure does the author use to convey the ideas and information about the history of Rosie the Riveter? Is this structure effective? Explain your thoughts.

_____

_____

_____

_____

_____

_____

_____

_____

_____

_____

_____

3. The author included an image in the report on pages 969. What purpose does this image serve? What other graphics, formatting, or multimedia elements could the author have used to help aid comprehension?

_____

_____

_____

_____

_____

_____

_____

_____

_____

_____

_____

Informative Text

W.9–10.2, a
W.9–10.2, b

APPLY WHAT YOU'VE LEARNED

4. As you conduct research on your topic, take notes on note cards (see page 964 of your textbook for more help). Using your notes, create an outline to help you develop an organization for your report. Include some of the facts, extended definitions, concrete details, quotations, or other information and examples that you will use to develop your topic.

Topic: _____

I. _____

    A. _____

    B. _____

    C. _____

II. _____

    A. _____

    B. _____

    C. _____

III. _____

    A. _____

    B. _____

    C. _____

IV. _____

    A. _____

    B. _____

    C. _____

5. What formatting (such as heads and subheads), graphics (such as charts or photos), and multimedia elements (such as video clips) will you use in your report to help aid comprehension?

_____

_____

_____

_____

_____

Informative Text

Use Transitions and Precise Language

Good writers use transitions, such as words, phrases, and clauses, to link sections of text and create a cohesive, or organized, report. Some common transitional words and phrases include *first, next, after, in a similar way, above all, then,* and *finally*. Transitions also help clarify the relationships among complex ideas.

Good writers also use precise language and domain-specific vocabulary to help make complex ideas easier for the reader to understand. For example, if you were writing a report about a scientific topic, such as refrigeration safety, you would want to use vocabulary specific to the topic, such as *vaporization, refrigerant,* and *compression*. These words are the most precise choices for the context.

LEARN FROM THE MODEL

Reread passages from "Rosie the Riveter: Everyday Hero" as indicated below and analyze how the author uses transitions and precise language.

1. Reread the report's first and second paragraphs on page 966. Identify three examples of precise or domain-specific language that relate to the events of World War II and the creation of Rosie the Riveter. How does this language help clarify the author's points?

   _____

   _____

   _____

   _____

   _____

   _____

   _____

2. What transitional word or phrase does the author use in the fourth paragraph on page 967? What purpose does this transition serve?

   _____

   _____

   _____

   _____

Informative Text

W.9–10.2, c
W.9–10.2, d

APPLY WHAT YOU'VE LEARNED

3. Review your outline on page 162. What words, phrases, or clauses would help make your transitions from point to point clear? Jot down several possible transitions below.

_____

_____

_____

_____

4. Pick one point from your outline and write a few sentences below using transitions to link this point to its support (such as facts, details, or quotations).

_____

_____

_____

_____

_____

_____

_____

Establish and Maintain an Appropriate Style and Tone

In an informative/explanatory text, it is important for writers to maintain a relatively formal style and an objective tone, or attitude, so that readers think the text is credible and unbiased. For example, if a writer is addressing the history of the Electoral College, it would not be appropriate for him or her to include a statement such as, "I think the Electoral College is stupid and should be replaced." The tone of the statement is subjective (it reflects the writer's personal opinion) and is presented too casually. The writer would sound more credible if he or she presented objective facts about the system, including its pros and cons.

LEARN FROM THE MODEL

Reread passages from "Rosie the Riveter: Everyday Hero" as indicated and analyze how the author establishes and maintains an appropriate style and tone.

1. Review the report's fifth and sixth paragraphs on pages 967–968. What words and phrases contribute to the formal style of the research report? How? Find at least two examples. Use the chart below to address these questions.

Word or Phrase	How It Contributes to Formal Style

2. How would you describe the tone, or attitude, of the entire report? Support your response with evidence from the text.

_____

_____

_____

_____

Informative Text

APPLY WHAT YOU'VE LEARNED

W.9–10.2, e

3. Look at your outline on page 162 and choose one paragraph to develop on the lines below. Focus on establishing and maintaining a formal style and an objective tone as you write.

_____

_____

_____

_____

_____

_____

_____

_____

_____

Provide a Conclusion

An effective conclusion in an informative/explanatory text should follow from and support the information or explanation that the writer has presented. Strong conclusions often present the significance of the topic or include a comment that ties the text to larger ideas.

LEARN FROM THE MODEL

Reread passages from "Rosie the Riveter: Everyday Hero" as indicated below and analyze how the author constructs an effective conclusion.

1. Reread the last paragraph of the report on page 968. How does this conclusion support the information that the writer presented in the rest of the text?

_____

_____

_____

_____

2. What final thought does the author leave with the reader? Is this an effective concluding statement? Why or why not?

_____

_____

_____

_____

_____

W.9–10.2, f | **APPLY WHAT YOU'VE LEARNED**

3. Use the lines below to jot down possible ideas for the conclusion of your report. How will the conclusion relate to the rest of your report? What final thought might you leave with the reader?

_____

_____

_____

_____

_____

_____

_____

_____

_____

_____

_____

_____

_____

_____

_____

_____

_____

Informative Text

Draft

W.9-10.10

Before you begin drafting, review your prewriting notes on pages 158–167. Then write your first draft on a computer, following the instructions below.

Write the Introduction

W.9-10.2, a, e

Begin by writing the introductory paragraph or paragraphs of your research report. Your introduction should

- grab the reader's attention (consider starting with an interesting anecdote, a surprising fact, or a thought-provoking question)
- introduce your topic
- present your thesis statement, or controlling idea
- establish a formal style and an objective tone

Write the Body

W.9-10.2, a
W.9-10.2, b
W.9-10.2, c
W.9-10.2, d
W.9-10.2, e
W.9-10.7
W.9-10.8

Write Cohesive Paragraphs Use your outline to guide you as you write the body of your report. Begin each paragraph with a topic sentence. Then develop your topic with well-chosen, relevant, and sufficient facts; extended definitions; concrete details; quotations; or other information and examples that are appropriate to your audience's knowledge of the topic. Integrate information into your report selectively to maintain the flow of ideas. Do not simply include every piece of information that you found on your topic. As you write, organize your ideas and information in a way that allows you to make important connections and distinctions between them. Synthesize multiple sources to demonstrate an understanding of your subject.

Use Transitions and Precise Language Use a variety of transitions to link major sections of text and help you clarify the relationships between ideas. Remember to use precise language and vocabulary that is specific to your topic. For example, if you are writing about the origins of haiku, you will want to mention literary elements such as imagery and figurative language that are specific to poetry and literature.

Use Formatting and Graphics As you write, remember to include formatting when appropriate (such as heads and subheads) to help guide your readers. Consider including graphics (such as tables, maps, or graphs) and/or multimedia elements (such as links to video clips) if they will help readers comprehend your topic.

Credit Your Sources As you write, maintain the formal style and objective tone that you established in the introduction. Avoid plagiarizing, or presenting an author's words or ideas as if they are your own. You must credit your sources not only for material directly quoted but also for any facts or ideas obtained from the source. Follow a standard format for your citations and include a Works Cited list at the end of your report. See pages R34–R37 in your textbook for more information.

Informative Text

Write the Conclusion

W.9–10.2, f

Finally, write the conclusion of your report. Make sure it follows from and supports the information or explanation you presented in your report. The conclusion should restate your thesis statement in a different way and summarize the main points in the report. You should try to end with a strong closing statement that leaves a lasting impression and articulates the significance of your topic.

Revise

W.9–10.4
W.9–10.5

To revise your research report, you will be focusing on the content, or the message, of your writing and possibly applying one or more of these four revision strategies:

- **add** details and information to make the message clearer
- **remove** distracting or unnecessary words or ideas
- **replace** bland or overused language with more precise or stronger words
- **rearrange** phrases and sentences to be sure the message is logically presented

The questions that follow will show you how to use these revision strategies. They will help you consider how well the development, organization, and style of your report are appropriate to task, purpose, and audience.

Focus and Coherence

Ask yourself the following questions. Then evaluate your report and check each box when your report meets the criteria.

☐ Does my report have a clear focus?

☐ Do all the parts work together so that I achieve my purpose?

Organization

W.9–10.2, a, f

Ask yourself the following questions. Then evaluate your report and check each box when your report meets the criteria.

☐ Does the beginning introduce my topic?

☐ Does the middle organize complex ideas, concepts, and information to make important connections and distinctions?

☐ Does the conclusion follow from and support the information or explanation I presented in the report?

Informative Text

Development of Ideas

W.9–10.2, b

Ask yourself the following questions. Then evaluate your report and check each box when your report meets the criteria.

☐ Does my report reflect a logical progression of ideas?

☐ Did I develop the topic with well-chosen, relevant, and sufficient facts; extended definitions; concrete details; quotations; or other information and examples that are appropriate to my audience's knowledge of the topic?

Voice—Word Choice

W.9–10.2, d
W.9–10.2, e
L.9–10.3

Ask yourself the following questions. Then evaluate your report and check each box when your report meets the criteria.

☐ Did I use precise language and domain-specific vocabulary?

☐ Did I apply knowledge of language to make effective choices for meaning or style?

☐ Did I establish and maintain a formal style and an objective tone?

Voice—Sentence Fluency

W.9–10.2, c

Ask yourself the following questions. Then evaluate your report and check each box when your report meets the criteria.

☐ Does my writing flow smoothly?

☐ Does my report include various transitions to link major sections of text, create cohesion, and clarify the relationships among complex ideas and concepts?

☐ Did I emphasize important points?

Edit and Proofread

Correct Errors in Grammar

L.9–10.3, a

Editing involves correcting errors in grammar, usage, mechanics, and spelling. As you edit, make sure your work conforms to the guidelines in a style manual that is appropriate for this type of writing. Check with your teacher to see which style guide you should use for reference.

Begin the editing stage by taking a careful look at your sentences. Make sure that each sentence expresses a complete thought in a way that is grammatically correct. Use the checklist that follows to edit your sentences.

Informative Text

SENTENCE-EDITING CHECKLIST

☐ Have I avoided sentence fragments?

☐ Have I avoided run-on sentences?

☐ Do verbs agree with their subjects?

☐ Are pronouns used correctly?

☐ Are verbs used correctly?

☐ Have I avoided misplaced and dangling modifiers?

☐ Have I used phrases and clauses correctly?

☐ Have I used parallel structure?

Correct Errors in Mechanics and Spelling

L.9–10.2, c

Next, check for and correct any errors in mechanics (punctuation and capitalization) and spelling.

Use the checklist below to edit your speech.

You should also use a dictionary to check and confirm spellings.

PROOFREADING CHECKLIST

☐ Are commas and other punctuation marks used as needed?

☐ Are all words spelled correctly?

☐ Are capital letters used as needed?

Present/Publish

W.9–10.6

After you have written and polished your research report, you will want to publish and present it. You may wish to consider some of these publishing and presenting options:

- Create a class anthology.
- Enter your report into a writing contest.
- Publish your report on the Internet.

Consider using technology, including the Internet, to publish your report, taking advantage of technology's capacity to display information flexibly and dynamically. You may wish to consult some of the projects in the Reading section of this book for additional publishing ideas that include technology.

Informative Text

Grammar Practice

Semicolons and Colons

L.9–10.2, a | A semicolon (;) joins different elements within a sentence. A colon (:) indicates that an example, explanation, restatement, or a quotation follows.

Semicolons Between Independent Clauses

You know that a comma and a coordinating conjunction (*and, but, or, for, yet,* or *so*) can be used to join independent, or main, clauses. When such clauses are closely connected, however, they may be joined by a semicolon instead.

> Until the early 1940s most women felt that their only job was caring for a home, but World War II changed that.

> Until the early 1940s most women felt that their only job was caring for a home; World War II changed that.

Independent clauses may, instead, be joined by a semicolon followed by a conjunctive adverb (such as *therefore, however,* or *nevertheless*). If this method is used, a comma must follow the conjunctive adverb.

> Rosie the Riveter was featured on posters during the war; therefore, she was given a look of strength and determination.

Independent clauses may also be joined by a semicolon followed by an expression such as *for example, in fact, on the contrary,* followed by a comma.

> Rosie the Riveter looked like a worker; for example, she had a tool in her hand.

Exercise A: Using Semicolons Between Independent Clauses

On the lines join the two clauses in the following items by inserting at least one each of the following: (1) a semicolon alone, (2) a semicolon with a conjunctive adverb followed by a comma, (3) a semicolon followed by an expression followed by a comma.

1. Millions of able-bodied men joined the armed services _____ workers were needed to replace them in heavy industry.

2. New jobs were created _____ arms factories had many openings.

3. Rosie was not manly in appearance _____ she was quite attractive.

4. She inspired new styles _____ slacks and bandanas became popular.

Informative Text

Colons to Introduce Lists

A colon often introduces a list of items, especially after such expressions as *these, the following,* or *as follows.* Do not use a colon to introduce a list if the list immediately follows a verb or a preposition.

Incorrect: Rosie the Riveter was: a symbol of strength, patriotism, and heroism.

Correct: Rosie the Riveter was a symbol of strength, patriotism, and heroism.

Correct: Rosie the Riveter was many things: a symbol of strength, patriotism, and heroism.

Exercise B: Using Colons to Introduce Lists

Are the following lists punctuated correctly or incorrectly? Write C or I on the line to identify the punctuation as correct or incorrect.

___**5.** During the war women met society's changes by: working outside the home, handling family finances, and mixing with people of different backgrounds.

___**6.** Women learned some new skills: welding, hammering, and riveting.

___**7.** The OWI challenged women to do their patriotic duty, share in the war effort, and "keep the home fires burning."

Colons to Introduce Quotations

A colon introduces a long or formal quotation in the same way as it introduces a list. A complete sentence following a colon is capitalized.

Incorrect: One recorded quotation was:
I learned a lot in those years. . . . I learned to look for a job. I learned to get along and mingle with people from different backgrounds.

Correct: One recorded quotation was "I learned a lot in those years. . . . I learned to look for a job. I learned to get along and mingle with people from different backgrounds."

Correct: One recorded quotation appeared as follows:
I learned a lot in those years. . . . I learned to look for a job. I learned to get along and mingle with people from different backgrounds.

Informative Text

Exercise C: Using Colons to Introduce Quotations

Do the colons in the following items introduce quotations correctly or incorrectly? Write **C** or **I** on the line to identify the punctuation as correct or incorrect.

___**8.** The Rosie on Norman Rockwell's famous 1943 cover was described as: "powerful, competent, and womanly."

___**9.** The Rosie in Norman Rockwell's famous cover was clearly described: "powerful, competent, and womanly."

___**10.** The Rosie in Norman Rockwell's famous cover was described this way: "powerful, competent, and womanly."

Check Your Writing

Check your research report for the use of semicolons and colons. Make sure you have used semicolons where they would be useful to link independent clauses. If you used conjunctive adverbs or expressions with semicolons preceding them, make sure you also used commas after those adverbs or expressions. Also check your report to make sure that, if you used colons to introduce quotations, you used them correctly.

Informative Text

Writing Workshop
AUTOBIOGRAPHICAL NARRATIVE

Glencoe Literature Connection: *from* Black Boy, pages 297–305

Before starting the lesson, read the following selections and complete the lesson activities in *Glencoe Literature*.

from Black Boy, by Richard Wright **(pages 297–305)**

In this lesson, you will study an excerpt from Richard Wright's *Black Boy* to discover how the author effectively uses the narrative writing methods and techniques listed below. You will then write your own autobiographical narrative using these methods and techniques. As you complete this workshop, you will practice the following standards:

W.9–10.3, a | **Engage and Orient the Reader**

- Set out a problem, situation, or observation.
- Establish one or multiple points of view.
- Introduce a narrator and/or characters.

W.9–10.3, a
W.9–10.3, c | **Sequence Events**

- Create a smooth progression of experiences or events.
- Sequence events so that they build on one another to create a coherent whole.

W.9–10.3, b
W.9–10.3, d | **Use Narrative Techniques**

- Use techniques such as dialogue, pacing, description, reflection, and multiple plot lines, to develop experiences, events, and/or characters.
- Use precise words and phrases, telling details, and sensory language to convey a vivid picture of the experiences, events, setting, and/or characters.

W.9–10.3, e | **Provide a Conclusion**

- Provide a conclusion that follows from and reflects on what is experienced, observed, or resolved over the course of the narrative.

Narrative

Analyze and Prewrite

Engage and Orient the Reader

Narrative writing is telling a story, whether the story is fictional or true. Good narrative writers engage and orient the reader by setting out a clear problem or situation, establishing a point or points of view, and introducing a narrator and/or main characters. In an autobiographical narrative the problem is related to a period or event in the writer's life, and the story is almost always told from the first-person point of view.

LEARN FROM THE MODEL

Reread the opening paragraphs on page 299 to see how Richard Wright engages and orients the reader in the excerpt from *Black Boy*.

1. What problem or situation does the narrator set out at the end of paragraph 2?

_____

_____

_____

2. Use the chart below to describe the narrator of *Black Boy*.

Narrator's Characteristics
Age:
Gender:
Appearance:
Feelings:

Narrative

3. What point of view does Wright use in this narrative? How can you tell?

_____

_____

_____

_____

_____

_____

4. How would you describe the narrator's attitude on this page? Support your response with at least two examples from the text.

_____

_____

_____

_____

_____

_____

_____

_____

| W.9–10.3, a |

APPLY WHAT YOU'VE LEARNED

5. What problem or conflict do you want to bring out in your narrative?

_____

_____

_____

_____

_____

_____

Narrative

6. Identify the period in your life you want to write about. What will be your age, situation, and personality? What thoughts and feelings will you want to depict? Write your responses in the chart below.

My Characteristics
Age:
Situation:
Personality:
Thoughts and Feelings:

7. From what point of view will you tell your narrative? Why?

_____

_____

_____

_____

_____

_____

_____

Narrative

Create a Coherent Sequence of Events and Conclusion

The story you tell about yourself should present a smooth progression of experiences or events. Good narrative writers use a variety of techniques to sequence events so that they build on one another to create a coherent whole. They also provide a conclusion that follows from and reflects on what is experienced, observed, or resolved over the course of the narrative.

LEARN FROM THE MODEL

Review the order of events and the ending in the excerpt from *Black Boy* to see how Richard Wright creates a coherent sequence and conclusion.

1. What problems does Wright encounter after he publishes his short story? Write your responses in the chart below using the headings given as a guide.

Reactions from Classmates:
Granny's Reaction:
His Mother's Reaction:
Uncle Tom's and Aunt Addie's Reactions:

Narrative

2. How do the events in the chart on the previous page follow a logical progression that creates a coherent, or organized, whole?

_____

_____

_____

_____

_____

3. How does Wright respond to the reactions his story gets? How is he changed by them?

_____

_____

_____

_____

_____

4. In commenting on these reactions, what conclusions does the narrator draw

- About his classmates?

_____

_____

_____

- About his state and country?

_____

_____

_____

- About himself as a boy and about his future?

_____

_____

_____

Narrative

W.9–10.3, a
W.9–10.3, c
W.9–10.3, e

APPLY WHAT YOU'VE LEARNED

5. What will be the sequence of events in your narrative? Use as many boxes as you need.

> **Event:**

> **Event:**

> **Event:**

> **Event:**

> **Event:**

> **Event:**

Narrative

6. What will connect these events to one another? How will this sequence of events create a coherent, or organized, whole?

_____

_____

_____

7. How will the conclusion of your narrative show how the events you write about have changed you or what you have learned from them?

_____

_____

_____

Use Narrative Techniques: Description

Description is a detailed portrayal of a person, place, or thing. Good writers use elements of description to convey a vivid picture of the setting, experiences, events, and characters or individuals in a narrative. These elements include

- precise words and phrases
- sensory language, or details that appeal to the five senses—touch, smell, sound, sight, and taste
- telling details, or concise and thoughtful particulars that tell the reader something important

LEARN FROM THE MODEL

Reread passages from *Black Boy* as indicated in the questions that follow and analyze how Richard Wright uses elements of description.

1. In the first paragraph, what precise words and phrases does Wright use to present the setting and to convey his attitude and outlook as a young student? How do these words help form your impression of Wright at this point in the narrative?

_____

_____

_____

_____

Narrative

2. In the third and fourth paragraphs, what sensory details, or imagery, does Wright include and to what senses do they appeal? From these details, what can you infer about Wright and about the editor?

_____

_____

_____

_____

3. Reread the last paragraph on page 300 and its continuation at the beginning of page 302. What details does Wright use to tell how his classmates viewed him? What do these details tell you about Wright's personality as a young student?

_____

_____

_____

_____

_____

W.9–10.3, b
W.9–10.3, d

APPLY WHAT YOU'VE LEARNED

4. On the following page, write sentences in which you describe and elaborate on how you and others look, think, act, feel, and interact at each point in your narrative. Refer to the excerpt from *Black Boy* to give you ideas and techniques. Be sure to include

- precise words and phrases
- sensory language, or details that appeal to the five senses—touch, smell, sound, sight, and taste
- telling details, or concise and thoughtful particulars that tell the reader something important

Refer to your sequence of events graphic organizer on page 181 as needed.

Narrative

Event/Situation:

_____

_____

_____

Interactions and Reactions of Those Involved:

_____

_____

_____

Event/Situation:

_____

_____

_____

Interactions and Reactions of Those Involved:

_____

_____

_____

Use Narrative Techniques: Dialogue and Pacing

Dialogue is the conversation between characters in a literary work. In an autobiographical narrative, dialogue brings to life the qualities and personalities of the people being described by showing what they are thinking and feeling as they react to others and to events. Dialogue can help create mood and develop theme.

Dialogue also advances a narrative's **plot**, or sequence of events, and is therefore a key element in a narrative's **pacing**, or the speed with which the action proceeds.

Narrative

LEARN FROM THE MODEL

Reread passages from *Black Boy* as indicated below and analyze how Richard Wright uses dialogue and pacing.

1. Reread the dialogue between Wright and the newspaper editor on pages 299–300. How does Wright's use of dialogue in this passage bring the two individuals and their interaction to life for you as a reader? Explain and provide examples to support your response.

_____

_____

_____

_____

_____

2. Reread the dialogue between Wright and his classmates in the second column on page 300. How does this dialogue further help to develop Wright's personality for you as a reader? What does the dialogue help you infer about Wright's classmates?

_____

_____

_____

_____

3. Describe the length of the sentences that Wright uses in the dialogue with his classmates. How does the sentence length affect the pacing of their conversation?

_____

_____

_____

_____

_____

Narrative

W.9–10.3, b **APPLY WHAT YOU'VE LEARNED**

4. Review your sentences on pages 177–178 in which you wrote descriptions of conflicts, situations, and individuals in your narrative. Write down key sections or parts of dialogue to show what those individuals are thinking and feeling as they react to others and to events and situations. Refer to the excerpt from *Black Boy* to give you ideas and techniques. Refer to your sequence of events graphic organizer on page 181 as needed.

_____

_____

_____

_____

_____

_____

_____

_____

Use Narrative Techniques: Reflection

Reflection is the inclusion of the thoughts, opinions, or attitudes of the author/narrator or of other individuals. Reflection can be included in dialogue or in descriptive or explanatory passages.

LEARN FROM THE MODEL

Reread passages from *Black Boy* as indicated in the questions that follow and analyze how Richard Wright includes reflection.

1. Reread the last paragraph of the mother's dialogue that begins at the bottom of the first column on page 302. What opinions or thoughts of the mother does this passage convey?

_____

_____

_____

_____

Narrative

2. Reread the last three paragraphs of Wright's narrative. What attitude toward the South does Wright convey in his reflection?

_____

_____

_____

_____

3. What metaphor, or comparison, does Wright include in the last paragraph? How does this metaphor help to convey Wright's attitude about his future?

_____

_____

_____

_____

W.9–10.3, b   **APPLY WHAT YOU'VE LEARNED**

4. Write notes about your own reflections on what you have experienced, observed, or resolved in the events of your narrative. Write notes showing how you will include reflection in dialogue, in your description of individuals' unspoken thoughts, or in your own commentary as the author/narrator.

_____

_____

_____

_____

_____

_____

_____

Narrative

Use Narrative Techniques: Multiple Plot Lines

Plot is the sequence of events in a narrative work. Most short narratives have a single plot line and are tightly crafted to build suspense. Longer narratives often have **multiple plot lines** and convey events that take place around various characters or individuals. Often a writer will construct a narrative so that one plot line is the central or dominant plot and the others are the minor or subplots. Plot lines can converge or can contrast with each other.

LEARN FROM THE MODEL

1. Reread the excerpt from *Black Boy* and map out the plot line. Most plots develop in five stages: exposition, rising action, climax, falling action, and resolution. Complete the graphic organizer below by summarizing the events that take place at each of the five stages of the plot in the excerpt from *Black Boy*.

Plot Line: Summary of Events
Exposition
Rising Action
Climax
Falling Action
Resolution

Narrative

W.9–10.3, b | **APPLY WHAT YOU'VE LEARNED**

2. Create one or two subplot lines to include in your narrative. Refer to the sequence of events chart on page 181 and build your subplot off of one of those events. Involve at least two individuals in your subplot. One or more of the individuals you feature in a subplot could be new to your narrative. Your subplot will be a sequence of events going on within your narrative as your main plot events take place. For ideas and techniques, refer to your completed Plot Line graphic organizer on the previous page and consider how Wright structured the plot in the excerpt from *Black Boy*. Follow a similar structure for your subplot line or lines.

Event from main plot line sequence:

Subplot Line Events and Stages

Exposition:

Rising Action:

Climax:

Falling Action:

Resolution:

Narrative

Draft

W.9–10.10 | Before you begin drafting, review your prewriting notes on pages 176–189. Then write your first draft on a computer, following the instructions below.

Write the Opening

W.9–10.3, a | Begin by writing the opening to your narrative. In the opening, you should introduce the conflict, or problem, and the people who are involved. You should also establish the point of view, which will most likely be first person since you are the narrator.

Add descriptive details about the people and events in your narrative from your prewriting notes.

Include Dialogue

W.9–10.3, b | As you write, include dialogue to help define the people and events, enhance the pacing, and move the plot along. Identify the purpose of the dialogue and the type of language you will use to convey each speaker's age, background, and personality. You will also want to communicate each speaker's thoughts and feelings.

Use tag lines (the words that identify the speaker, such as "said Charlie") to identify each speaker. Avoid using "said" repeatedly in tag lines, and instead use a variety of descriptive words, such as *answered, asked, replied, screamed, shouted, murmured, whispered.*

Write the Body

W.9–10.3, b, c, d | Next, use your prewriting notes to write the body of your narrative. Remember to

- use descriptive details to develop people and events
- pace the sequence of events you have mapped out so that events build on one another to create a coherent whole
- use narrative techniques, such as dialogue, to develop experiences, events, and/or people
- use precise words and phrases, telling details, and sensory language to convey a vivid picture of the experiences, events, setting, and/or people.

Write the Ending

W.9–10.3, e | Finally, write the ending of your narrative. Make sure that your ending follows from and reflects on what you experience, observe, or resolve over the course of the narrative.

Narrative

Revise

W.9–10.4
W.9–10.5

To revise your narrative, you will be focusing on the content, or the message, of your writing and possibly applying one or more of these four revision strategies:

- **add** details and information to make the message clearer
- **remove** distracting or unnecessary words or ideas
- **replace** bland or overused language with more precise or stronger words
- **rearrange** phrases and sentences to be sure the message is logically presented

The questions that follow will show you how to use these revision strategies. They will help you consider how well the development, organization, and style of your narrative are appropriate to task, purpose, and audience.

Focus and Coherence

Ask yourself the following questions. Then evaluate your narrative and check each box when your narrative meets the criteria.

☐ Does my narrative have a clear focus?

☐ Do all the parts work together so that I achieve my purpose?

☐ Will readers be able to follow the sequence of events?

Organization

W.9–10.3, a
W.9–10.3, c
W.9–10.3, e

Ask yourself the following questions. Then evaluate your narrative and check each box when your narrative meets the criteria.

☐ Does the beginning introduce the people, conflict, and point of view?

☐ Does the middle use a variety of techniques to sequence events so that they build to create a coherent whole?

☐ Does the ending follow from and reflect on what is experienced, observed, or resolved over the course of the narrative?

Development of Ideas

W.9–10.3, b

Ask yourself the following questions. Then evaluate your narrative and check each box when your narrative meets the criteria.

☐ Are the people fully developed?

☐ Are they presented in an interesting, believable, and meaningful way?

☐ Do I use narrative techniques, such as dialogue, pacing, description, reflection, and multiple plot lines, to develop experiences, events, and/or people?

Narrative

Voice—Word Choice

W.9–10.3, d
L.9–10.3

Ask yourself the following questions. Then evaluate your narrative and check each box when your narrative meets the criteria.

☐ Does my writing include precise words and phrases and telling details to convey a vivid picture of the experiences, events, setting, and/or people?

☐ Does my narrative include sensory language?

Voice—Sentence Fluency

Ask yourself the following questions. Then evaluate your narrative and check each box when your narrative meets the criteria.

☐ Do the sentences vary in length and structure?

☐ Does my writing flow smoothly?

☐ Have I emphasized important points?

Edit and Proofread

Correct Errors in Grammar

Editing involves correcting errors in grammar, usage, mechanics, and spelling.

Begin the editing stage by taking a careful look at your sentences. Make sure that each sentence expresses a complete thought in a way that is grammatically correct. Use the checklist below to edit your sentences.

SENTENCE-EDITING CHECKLIST

☐ Have I avoided sentence fragments?

☐ Have I avoided run-on sentences?

☐ Do verbs agree with their subjects?

☐ Are pronouns used correctly?

☐ Are verbs used correctly?

☐ Have I avoided misplaced and dangling modifiers?

☐ Have I used phrases and clauses correctly?

☐ Have I used parallel construction?

Narrative

Correct Errors in Mechanics and Spelling

L.9–10.2, c Next, check for and correct any errors in mechanics (punctuation and capitalization) and spelling.

Use the checklist on the next page to edit your narrative.

You should also use a dictionary to check and confirm spellings.

PROOFREADING CHECKLIST

☐ Are commas and other punctuation marks used as needed?

☐ Are all words spelled correctly?

☐ Are capital letters used as needed?

Present/Publish

W.9–10.6 After you have polished your narrative, you will want to publish and present it. You may wish to consider some of these publishing and presenting options:

- create a class anthology
- publish your narrative in an online forum or magazine
- enter your narrative into a writing contest
- perform your narrative as readers' theater

Consider using technology to publish your narrative, taking advantage of technology's capacity to display information flexibly and dynamically.

Grammar Practice

Parallel Construction

L.9–10.1, a Words and groups of words that have the same form and function within a sentence are **parallel.**

> **Parallel:** Writers must know how to <u>construct</u> and <u>punctuate sentences</u>.

The underlined words and phrases in the sentence above are parallel because they have the same form (infinitive verb, or *to* verb) and serve the same function (to convey action) within the sentence.

Errors in parallelism often occur within lists.

> **Not Parallel:** <u>Writing</u> and <u>to travel north</u> were Wright's dreams.

> **Parallel:** <u>Writing and traveling north</u> were Wright's dreams.

Notice that the list of activities in the second sentence above has parallel construction. The underlined words have the same form (gerund, or *-ing* verbal) and serve the same function (subject) within the sentence.

arrative

When creating parallel construction, you should use a preposition (*around, at, by, from, to*) to introduce every activity or item or only the first activity or item.

Not Parallel: Wright hoped for approval <u>from the editor, his friends</u>, and <u>from his teachers</u>.

Parallel: Wright hoped for approval <u>from the editor, from his friends</u>, and <u>from his teachers</u>.

Parallel: Wright hoped for approval <u>from the editor, his friends</u>, and <u>his teachers</u>.

Exercise: Correcting Errors in Parallel Construction

Rewrite each sentence on the lines provided, correcting errors in parallelism.

1. Wright's friends were confused about his writing, his desires, and about his hopes for the future.

_____

_____

2. His friends showed confusion by asking questions and did not understand his answers.

_____

_____

3. Only the editor understood that fiction is not lies and was liking Wright's story.

_____

_____

4. Wright hoped to move north, finding new opportunities, and to meet people more like himself.

_____

_____

Check Your Writing

Check your autobiographical narrative for parallel construction. If words or groups of words within sentences are not parallel, correct them. Parallel construction will make your narrative flow better.

Narrative

Vocabulary

L.9–10.4, a
L.9–10.4, c

Context as Clues to Meaning

Skilled readers often use context clues to determine the meaning of an unfamiliar word. **Context clues** are the words, phrases, and sentences surrounding an unfamiliar word that provide hints about its meaning. There are different types of context clues you can look for, including those that involve word relationships, description or contrast, examples, and general reasoning.

Sometimes context clues may only provide a general sense of what an unfamiliar word means. You may need to consult print or digital resources, such as a dictionary or glossary, to check the word's precise meaning.

L.9–10.4
L9–10.4, a
L9–10.4, d
L9–10.5
L9–10.6

Context Clues: Word Relationships

Context clues that involve synonyms or antonyms are among the more common kinds. For example, "The performance was <u>mediocre</u>, and I had expected it to be much better than merely passable." In this sentence, *mediocre* and *passable* appear to be synonyms and to share a meaning of "ordinary." Likewise, "He not only didn't try to encourage me; he tried to <u>dissuade</u> me" suggests that *dissuade* means "discourage" by providing a contrast to *encourage*.

Exercise A: Using Context Clues—Word Relationships

Use context clues to guess the meaning of the underlined word in each item. Circle the letter of the word's likely meaning. Remember to check each guess.

1. Completing the job required <u>sundry</u> skills, and our group did not possess the various abilities necessary.

    a. rare
    b. several
    c. basic
    d. high-level

2. I did not expect <u>ignominious</u> behavior from an honorable person.

    a. stubborn
    b. confusing
    c. shameful
    d. upstanding

3. She <u>manifested</u> how much she disliked the task, showing it in many ways.

    a. hid
    b. exaggerated
    c. ignored
    d. displayed

4. His illness was rare, but the doctor knew how to treat the man's <u>malady</u>.

    a. disease
    b. bad behavior
    c. pharmacy
    d. experiment

5. I awaken feeling lively. My sister, on the other hand, is <u>sluggish</u> for a long time after she gets up.

    a. active
    b. angry
    c. wide-awake
    d. slow-moving

L.9–10.4
L.9–10.4, a
L.9–10.4, d
L.9–10.6

Context Clues: Description or Contrast

Context clues sometimes provide description or contrast. For example, "She showed <u>solicitude</u> toward the frightened child, and this caring attention helped calm the boy."

Context clues may also provide contrast. For example, "I expected <u>sagacity</u> from Harry. Instead, he showed extremely poor judgment and a complete lack of sense." The contrast provided by "poor judgment" and "lack of sense" suggests that it means something similar to "wisdom."

Exercise B: Using Context Clues—Description and Contrast

Use context clues to guess the meaning of the underlined word in each item. Circle the letter of the word's likely meaning. Remember to check each guess.

6. Although there had once been great <u>rancor</u> between them, now they liked each other quite a bit and were the best of friends.

   a. curiosity   **c.** similarity
   b. hostility   **d.** understanding

7. We weren't able to completely <u>eradicate</u> the stains; some evidence of them remained.

   a. fade   **c.** erase
   b. darken   **d.** replace

8. He spent so much on luxuries and wastefulness that he went from having plenty of money to a state of complete <u>indigence</u>.

   a. poverty   **c.** rage
   b. cautiousness   **d.** wealth

9. I felt shaky and tired from my illness and much too <u>debilitated</u> to make it up the four flights of stairs.

   a. sad   **c.** lazy
   b. weak   **d.** irritable

10. I would have given anything I owned to have that sweater. I really <u>coveted</u> it.

   a. desired   **c.** bought
   b. noticed   **d.** admired

Vocabulary

L.9–10.4
L.9–10.4, a
L.9–10.4, d
L. 9–10.6

Context Clues: Examples

Sometimes you can figure out what an unfamiliar word means by paying attention to examples provided by context clues. For example, "Lemonade, iced tea, and punch were the only <u>potables</u> available at the party." The examples given by the sentence suggest that *potables* are beverages.

Exercise C: Using Context Clues—Examples

Use context clues to guess the meaning of the underlined word in each item. Circle the letter of the word's likely meaning. Remember to check each guess.

11. Their <u>avocations</u> included golf, playing the guitar, collecting baseball cards, and knitting.

   a. jobs   **c.** hobbies
   b. sports   **d.** creative activities

12. She had three <u>abodes</u>: a cabin in the mountains and a cottage by the ocean as well as an apartment in the city, where she spent most of the year.

   a. places to live   **c.** vacation spots
   b. work locations   **d.** sources of income

13. Wolves, bears, eagles, and lions are all <u>predatory</u> animals, but mountain goats, deer, cows, and squirrels are not.

   a. wild   **c.** social
   b. hunting   **d.** furry

14. The Pentagon, which has 17 miles of hallways, and the Willis Tower, which is more than 100 stories tall, are both <u>gargantuan</u> buildings.

   a. local   **c.** beautiful
   b. made of brick   **d.** extremely large

15. Raisins and peas are <u>diminutive</u> foods that a child is unlikely to choke on, but grapes should be cut in half.

   a. soft   **c.** healthy
   b. very small   **d.** skinless

L.9–10.4
L.9–10.4, a
L.9–10.4, d
L.9–10.6

Context Clues: General Reasoning

Even when context clues don't fall into a particular category, you may still be able to figure out a word's meaning just by using your own knowledge and reasoning. For example, look at this sentence: "She was acting as <u>obstinate</u> as a mule." Because you remember that mules are well-known for their stubbornness, you can easily guess that *obstinate* means something like "stubborn."

Exercise D: Using Context Clues—General Reasoning

Use context clues to guess the meaning of the underlined word. Circle the letter of the word's likely meaning. Remember to check each guess.

16. Eating right and getting plenty of exercise resulted in my feeling <u>robust</u>.

    a. smart   **c.** tired
    b. strong   **d.** cheerful

17. Shrieks of laughter and blaring music from next door made it clear that the neighbors' party was going to be a <u>boisterous</u> one.

    a. long   **c.** loud
    b. enjoyable   **d.** amusing

18. A stern glance from Dad as I began to speak was all that was necessary to <u>preclude</u> my interruption of his scolding.

    a. prevent   **c.** clarify
    b. encourage   **d.** intensify

19. We were able to find our way down the dark path because of the <u>luminosity</u> of the moon.

    a. size   **c.** position
    b. radiance   **d.** a covering

20. Instead of providing any explanation or details, she simply gave me the <u>succinct</u> answer "No, thanks."

    a. confusing   **c.** grumpy
    b. rude and selfish   **d.** brief and clear

Vocabulary

Patterns of Word Changes

In addition to using context clues, skilled readers often rely on two other strategies for determining the meaning of an unfamiliar word. The first strategy requires examining the suffix of an unfamiliar word. The second involves making connections between an unfamiliar word and related words that you already know. Both of these strategies require that you recognize patterns of word changes.

How Suffixes Affect Meaning

L.9–10.4
L.9–10.4, b
L.9–10.4, c
L.9–10.6

A **suffix** is a word part added to the end of a base word or a root that modifies, or changes, its meaning. Some suffixes modify a word's meaning very slightly. These include suffixes that change the number of a noun (*-s, -es; apples, benches*), the tense of a verb (*-d, -ed, -ing; sprinkled, snowed, thundering*), and the degree of comparison of an adjective (*-er, -est; colder, coldest*).

Many other suffixes, however, change the part of speech of a word and greatly affect meaning. For example, when the suffix *-ment* is added to a base word or root it forms a noun, as in *merriment, announcement,* and *amazement.* Similarly, when the suffix *-less* is added to a base word or root, it forms an adjective, as in *friendless, hopeless,* and *fearless.*

Often, you can unlock the meaning of unfamilar words by applying your knowledge of common suffixes. You may check your understanding of unfamiliar words by consulting print or digital resources, such as a dictionary or glossary.

Exercise A: Using Suffixes to Determine Meaning

Draw lines to separate each underlined word into two parts—a base word and a suffix. Then determine the meaning of the word by using your knowledge of suffixes. Circle the letter of the correct answer.

1. If you were looking for a place of <u>concealment</u>, you would want a place to

    a. hide   **b.** sleep   **c.** study

2. A <u>baseless</u> accusation is one that cannot be

    a. argued   **b.** stopped   **c.** supported

3. One place that exists for the purpose of <u>detainment</u> is a

    a. jail   **b.** library   **c.** gymnasium

4. <u>Mindless</u> activities are those that require no

    a. energy   **b.** effort   **c.** thinking

5. A <u>featureless</u> landscape is one that has no

    a. face   **b.** dangers   **c.** characteristics

Vocabulary

Noun-Forming Suffixes	Examples
-ation	realization, accusation
-ity	community, reality
Verb-Forming Suffixes	**Examples**
-ate	decorate, navigate
-ize	criticize, dramatize
Adjective-Forming Suffixes	**Examples**
-able / *-ible*	adorable, horrible
-ative / *-ive*	informative, active

Not all suffixes are as familiar as *-ment* and *-less*. The chart above presents other suffixes and tells how they affect the part of speech of the base word or root.

Keep in mind that not every word that ends with one of the suffixes shown above is necessarily the part of speech indicated. For example, *affectionate* is an adjective, not a noun.

It is also important to remember that adding a suffix may modify a base word's spelling. *Registration,* for example, comes from *register,* and *descriptive* comes from *describe.*

Exercise B: Using Suffixes to Determine Part of Speech and Meaning

Use the suffix chart and your knowledge of base words and roots to answer the following questions. (Remember that adding a suffix may modify a base word's spelling.) Write your answers on the lines provided.

6. What part of speech is <u>adaptation</u> most likely to be?

   _____

   _____

7. <u>Adaptive</u> behavior is that which allows an organism to

   _____

   _____

Vocabulary

8. What part of speech is <u>defensive</u> most likely to be?

_____

_____

9. A <u>defensible</u> statement is one that can be

_____

_____

10. What part of speech is <u>authenticate</u> most likely to be?

_____

_____

11. To prove the <u>authenticity</u> of an object establishes that it is

_____

_____

12. What part of speech is <u>equality</u> most likely to be?

_____

_____

13. If you <u>equalize</u> several things, you make them

_____

_____

14. What part of speech is <u>immobility</u> most likely to be?

_____

_____

15. If heavy rains <u>immobilize</u> airplanes, they make the airplanes

_____

_____

16. What part of speech is <u>illustrate</u> most likely to be?

_____

_____

Vocabulary

17. If you clarify your idea through <u>illustration</u>, you offer

_____

_____

18. What part of speech is <u>indisputable</u> most likely to be?

_____

_____

Using What You Know

When you learn a word, you also learn something about other words connected to it. For example, when you learned the meaning of *pronounce*, you also learned a great deal about *pronunciation, pronounceable, unpronounceable, mispronounce, mispronunciation,* and *pronouncement.*

Most words have connections to other words, and you can use those connections:

> *benevolent* contains the root *bene*
>
> *bene* is part of *benefit*, which is something good or helpful
>
> *benevolent* has something to do with goodness or helpfulness

If you use reasoning like this, you will find that you can get a good idea of the meanings of many words that are related to words you know. If getting a general idea of a word's meaning isn't sufficient, use online or digital resources, such as a dictionary or glossary, to find out its precise meaning.

Exercise C: Using Familiar Words to Determine Meanings of Unfamiliar Words

For each item, use what you know about the italicized word to figure out the meaning of the underlined word. Circle the letter of the correct answer.

19. By thinking about *combat*, you can tell that a <u>combative</u> person is likely to

    a. learn   **b.** fight   **c.** sleep

20. By thinking about *malnutrition*, you can tell that something that is <u>malodorous</u>

    a. smells bad   **b.** smells good   **c.** has no smell

21. By thinking about *error*, you can tell that to <u>err</u> is to make a

    a. fuss   **b.** mess   **c.** mistake

Vocabulary

22. By thinking about *provoke*, you can tell that a <u>provocation</u> is something that

    a. angers or irritates   **b.** grows larger   **c.** reveals what is hidden

23. By thinking about *sufficient*, you can tell that something that would <u>suffice</u> for a hungry person would be

    a. a big meal   **b.** a small snack   **c.** the aroma of baking

L.9–10.4
L.9–10.4, b
L.9–10.4, c
L.9–10.6

How Meanings Change

The meanings of words change over time. For example, the original meaning of *lady* was "one who kneads bread." The meaning we know today of "adult female" didn't come into use until the late 1800s. In the meantime, it went through a number of changes including "a woman of high social standing" and "a woman of refinement," both of which are still dictionary meanings for the word. "One who kneads bread," however, has disappeared from the dictionary.

We often learn one meaning of a word, such as *steel,* and then come across it in a context where the meaning we know doesn't make sense, such as "She had to steel herself to try out for the play." Only by considering a somewhat figurative meaning for *steel* as a verb would we ever guess that "to steel oneself" is "to make oneself strong, like steel." That definition, although not the original definition of steel, is now in dictionaries. It was used figuratively so often that it became, through common usage, not figurative at all.

Some words start off with figurative meanings. For example, a tightfisted person is merely stingy; his or her fists are not actually any tighter than anyone else's.

When you come across a word you know or a compound word made up of familiar words, but the meaning or meanings you know don't make sense, try thinking of a meaning that may have been added over time—a more figurative one.

Exercise D: Understanding Related Meanings

For each item, think about a meaning or meanings you know in order to guess the meaning of the underlined word. Circle the letter of the correct answer.

24. By thinking about the meanings you know for *cut* and *throat*, you could guess that if a competition is described as <u>cutthroat</u>, it is

    a. balanced   **b.** ruthless   **c.** quite uneven

25. By thinking about the meanings you know for *under* and *mine*, you could guess to <u>undermine</u> someone else's efforts would

    a. weaken them   **b.** support them   **c.** gives them more value

Vocabulary

26. By thinking about the meaning you know for *bite*, you could guess that a <u>biting</u> remark is one that

    a. is short   **b.** puzzles   **c.** wounds

27. By thinking about the meaning you know for *distant*, you could guess that a person who behaves *distantly* towards you seems

    a. unfriendly   **b.** worried   **c.** eager to talk

28. By thinking about the meaning you know for *stir*, you could guess that creating a <u>stir</u> would result in

    a. boredom   **b.** tidiness   **c.** excitement

29. By thinking about the meaning you know for *initial*, you could guess that a person's <u>initial</u> reaction is his or her

    a. spoken one   **b.** very first one   **c.** most lasting one

30. By thinking about the meaning you know for *close*, you could guess that when something reaches <u>closure</u>, it

    a. begins   **b.** comes to an end   **c.** becomes complicated

Vocabulary

Synonyms: Nuances

Synonyms are words that mean either the same or almost the same thing. There are, for example, small but important differences in the meanings of the synonyms *achy, sore, painful, uncomfortable, irritated, tender, burning,* and *agonizing*. These fine distinctions in the meanings of synonyms are called **nuances.** They are also often referred to as "shades of meaning."

L.9–10.5
L.9–10.5, b

Recognizing Nuances

Some synonyms differ from each other in their degree of intensity or in how positive or how negative they are. For example, *cold* and *freezing* are synonyms, but *freezing* means "very cold." Similarly, *foolish* and *silly* are synonyms, but *foolish* is more negative than *silly*.

Exercise A: Recognizing Nuances

Answer the following questions on the lines provided. You may use a print or digital dictionary if you are unsure of the answer.

1. How is <u>remind</u> different from <u>nag</u>?

   _____

   _____

2. How is <u>wretched</u> different from <u>unhappy</u>?

   _____

   _____

3. How is <u>pig-headed</u> different from <u>stubborn</u>?

   _____

   _____

4. How is <u>proud</u> different from <u>conceited</u>?

   _____

   _____

5. How is <u>shatter</u> different from <u>break</u>?

   _____

   _____

Vocabulary

L.9–10.4c
L.9–10.5, b

Analyzing Nuances

To avoid using a word that communicates an unintended meaning, you must make sure that your choice of a synonym is correct. Unless you know precisely what a word means, you must check it in a print or digital dictionary.

Exercise B: Analyzing Nuances

Read the synonyms for each word given below and then answer the questions about them. Do not use the same answer for more than one question. You may use a dictionary if you are unsure of the answer.

large: big, hefty, gigantic, generous, excessive

walk: stride, wander, trudge, strut, waddle

6. Which synonym for *large* means most exactly the same thing with no additional meaning? _____

7. Which synonym for *large* communicates that what is being described is extremely large? _____

8. Which synonym for *large* communicates that what is being described is too large or too much? _____

9. Which synonym for *large* communicates that what is being described is more than enough but not too much? _____

10. Which synonym for *large* communicates that what is being described is heavy as well as large? _____

11. Which synonym for *walk* communicates that the action is determined and somewhat rapid? _____

12. Which synonym for *walk* communicates that the action is slow and awkward? _____

13. Which synonym for *walk* communicates that the action is aimless? _____

14. Which synonym for *walk* communicates that the action shows self-congratulation? _____

15. Which synonym for *walk* communicates that the action is slow, tiring, and difficult? _____

Vocabulary

Grades 9–10 Common Core State Standards

Grades 9–10 Common Core State Standards

Reading Standards for Literature

Key Ideas and Details

1. Cite strong and thorough textual evidence to support analysis of what the text says explicitly as well as inferences drawn from the text.

2. Determine a theme or central idea of a text and analyze in detail its development over the course of the text, including how it emerges and is shaped and refined by specific details; provide an objective summary of the text.

3. Analyze how complex characters (e.g., those with multiple or conflicting motivations) develop over the course of a text, interact with other characters, and advance the plot or develop the theme.

Craft and Structure

4. Determine the meaning of words and phrases as they are used in the text, including figurative and connotative meanings; analyze the cumulative impact of specific word choices on meaning and tone (e.g., how the language evokes a sense of time and place; how it sets a formal or informal tone).

5. Analyze how an author's choices concerning how to structure a text, order events within it (e.g., parallel plots), and manipulate time (e.g., pacing, flashbacks) create such effects as mystery, tension, or surprise.

6. Analyze a particular point of view or cultural experience reflected in a work of literature from outside the United States, drawing on a wide reading of world literature.

Integration of Knowledge and Ideas

7. Analyze the representation of a subject or a key scene in two different artistic mediums, including what is emphasized or absent in each treatment (e.g., Auden's "Musée des Beaux Arts" and Breughel's *Landscape with the Fall of Icarus*).

8. (Not applicable to literature)

9. Analyze how an author draws on and transforms source material in a specific work (e.g., how Shakespeare treats a theme or topic from Ovid or the Bible or how a later author draws on a play by Shakespeare).

Range of Reading and Level of Text Complexity

10. By the end of grade 9, read and comprehend literature, including stories, dramas, and poems, in the grades 9–10 text complexity band proficiently, with scaffolding as needed at the high end of the range. By the end of grade 10, read and comprehend literature, including stories, dramas, and poems, at the high end of the grades 9–10 text complexity band independently and proficiently.

Reading Standards for Informational Text

Key Ideas and Details

1. Cite strong and thorough textual evidence to support analysis of what the text says explicitly as well as inferences drawn from the text.

2. Determine a central idea of a text and analyze its development over the course of the text, including how it emerges and is shaped and refined by specific details; provide an objective summary of the text.

3. Analyze how the author unfolds an analysis or series of ideas or events, including the order in which the points are made, how they are introduced and developed, and the connections that are drawn between them.

Craft and Structure

4. Determine the meaning of words and phrases as they are used in a text, including figurative, connotative, and technical meanings; analyze the cumulative impact of specific word choices on meaning and tone (e.g., how the language of a court opinion differs from that of a newspaper).

5. Analyze in detail how an author's ideas or claims are developed and refined by particular sentences, paragraphs, or larger portions of a text (e.g., a section or chapter).

6. Determine an author's point of view or purpose in a text and analyze how an author uses rhetoric to advance that point of view or purpose.

Integration of Knowledge and Ideas

7. Analyze various accounts of a subject told in different mediums (e.g., a person's life story in both print and multimedia), determining which details are emphasized in each account.

8. Delineate and evaluate the argument and specific claims in a text, assessing whether the reasoning is valid and the evidence is relevant and sufficient; identify false statements and fallacious reasoning.

9. Analyze seminal U.S. documents of historical and literary significance (e.g., Washington's Farewell Address, the Gettysburg Address, Roosevelt's Four Freedoms speech, King's "Letter from Birmingham Jail"), including how they address related themes and concepts.

Range of Reading and Level of Text Complexity

10. By the end of grade 9, read and comprehend literary nonfiction in the grades 9–10 text complexity band proficiently, with scaffolding as needed at the high end of the range. By the end of grade 10, read and comprehend literary nonfiction at the high end of the grades 9–10 text complexity band independently and proficiently.

Writing Standards

Text Types and Purposes

1. Write arguments to support claims in an analysis of substantive topics or texts, using valid reasoning and relevant and sufficient evidence.

   a. Introduce precise claim(s), distinguish the claim(s) from alternate or opposing claims, and create an organization that establishes clear relationships among claim(s), counterclaims, reasons, and evidence.

   b. Develop claim(s) and counterclaims fairly, supplying evidence for each while pointing out the strengths and limitations of both in a manner that anticipates the audience's knowledge level and concerns.

   c. Use words, phrases, and clauses to link the major sections of the text, create cohesion, and clarify the relationships between claim(s) and reasons, between reasons and evidence, and between claim(s) and counterclaims.

   d. Establish and maintain a formal style and objective tone while attending to the norms and conventions of the discipline in which they are writing.

   e. Provide a concluding statement or section that follows from and supports the argument presented.

2. Write informative/explanatory texts to examine and convey complex ideas, concepts, and information clearly and accurately through the effective selection, organization, and analysis of content.

   a. Introduce a topic; organize complex ideas, concepts, and information to make important connections and distinctions; include formatting (e.g., headings), graphics (e.g., figures, tables), and multimedia when useful to aiding comprehension.

   b. Develop the topic with well-chosen, relevant, and sufficient facts, extended definitions, concrete details, quotations, or other information and examples appropriate to the audience's knowledge of the topic.

   c. Use appropriate and varied transitions to link the major sections of the text, create cohesion, and clarify the relationships among complex ideas and concepts.

   d. Use precise language and domain-specific vocabulary to manage the complexity of the topic.

   e. Establish and maintain a formal style and objective tone while attending to the norms and conventions of the discipline in which they are writing.

   f. Provide a concluding statement or section that follows from and supports the information or explanation presented (e.g., articulating implications or the significance of the topic).

3. Write narratives to develop real or imagined experiences or events using effective technique, well-chosen details, and well-structured event sequences.

   a. Engage and orient the reader by setting out a problem, situation, or observation, establishing one or multiple point(s) of view, and introducing a narrator and/or characters; create a smooth progression of experiences or events.

   b. Use narrative techniques, such as dialogue, pacing, description, reflection, and multiple plot lines, to develop experiences, events, and/or characters.

   c. Use a variety of techniques to sequence events so that they build on one another to create a coherent whole.

   d. Use precise words and phrases, telling details, and sensory language to convey a vivid picture of the experiences, events, setting, and/or characters.

   e. Provide a conclusion that follows from and reflects on what is experienced, observed, or resolved over the course of the narrative.

Production and Distribution of Writing

4. Produce clear and coherent writing in which the development, organization, and style are appropriate to task, purpose, and audience. (Grade-specific expectations for writing types are defined in standards 1–3 above.)

5. Develop and strengthen writing as needed by planning, revising, editing, rewriting, or trying a new approach, focusing on addressing what is most significant for a specific purpose and audience.

6. Use technology, including the Internet, to produce, publish, and update individual or shared writing products, taking advantage of technology's capacity to link to other information and to display information flexibly and dynamically.

Research to Build and Present Knowledge

7. Conduct short as well as more sustained research projects to answer a question (including a self-generated question) or solve a problem; narrow or broaden the inquiry when appropriate; synthesize multiple sources on the subject, demonstrating understanding of the subject under investigation.

8. Gather relevant information from multiple authoritative print and digital sources, using advanced searches effectively; assess the usefulness of each source in answering the research question; integrate information into the text selectively to maintain the flow of ideas, avoiding plagiarism and following a standard format for citation.

9. Draw evidence from literary or informational texts to support analysis, reflection, and research.

   a. Apply *grades 9–10 Reading standards* to literature (e.g., "Analyze how an author draws on and transforms source material in a specific work [e.g., how Shakespeare treats a theme or topic from Ovid or the Bible or how a later author draws on a play by Shakespeare]").

   b. Apply *grades 9–10 Reading standards* to literary nonfiction (e.g., "Delineate and evaluate the argument and specific claims in a text, assessing whether the reasoning is valid and the evidence is relevant and sufficient; identify false statements and fallacious reasoning").

Range of Writing

10. Write routinely over extended time frames (time for research, reflection, and revision) and shorter time frames (a single sitting or a day or two) for a range of tasks, purposes, and audiences.

Speaking and Listening Standards

Comprehension and Collaboration

1. Initiate and participate effectively in a range of collaborative discussions (one-on-one, in groups, and teacher-led) with diverse partners on grades 9–10 topics, texts, and issues, building on others' ideas and expressing their own clearly and persuasively.

   a. Come to discussions prepared, having read and researched material under study; explicitly draw on that preparation by referring to evidence from texts and other research on the topic or issue to stimulate a thoughtful, well-reasoned exchange of ideas.

   b. Work with peers to set rules for collegial discussions and decision-making (e.g., informal consensus, taking votes on key issues, presentation of alternate views), clear goals and deadlines, and individual roles as needed.

   c. Propel conversations by posing and responding to questions that relate the current discussion to broader themes or larger ideas; actively incorporate others into the discussion; and clarify, verify, or challenge ideas and conclusions.

   d. Respond thoughtfully to diverse perspectives, summarize points of agreement and disagreement, and, when warranted, qualify or justify their own views and understanding and make new connections in light of the evidence and reasoning presented.

2. Integrate multiple sources of information presented in diverse media or formats (e.g., visually, quantitatively, orally) evaluating the credibility and accuracy of each source.

3. Evaluate a speaker's point of view, reasoning, and use of evidence and rhetoric, identifying any fallacious reasoning or exaggerated or distorted evidence.

Presentation of Knowledge and Ideas

4. Present information, findings, and supporting evidence clearly, concisely, and logically such that listeners can follow the line of reasoning and the organization, development, substance, and style are appropriate to purpose, audience, and task.

5. Make strategic use of digital media (e.g., textual, graphical, audio, visual, and interactive elements) in presentations to enhance understanding of findings, reasoning, and evidence and to add interest.

6. Adapt speech to a variety of contexts and tasks, demonstrating command of formal English when indicated or appropriate.

Language Standards

Conventions of Standard English

1. Demonstrate command of the conventions of standard English grammar and usage when writing or speaking.
   a. Use parallel structure.
   b. Use various types of phrases (noun, verb, adjectival, adverbial, participial, prepositional, absolute) and clauses (independent, dependent; noun, relative, adverbial) to convey specific meanings and add variety and interest to writing or presentations.

2. Demonstrate command of the conventions of standard English capitalization, punctuation, and spelling when writing.
   a. Use a semicolon (and perhaps a conjunctive adverb) to link two or more closely related independent clauses.
   b. Use a colon to introduce a list or quotation.
   c. Spell correctly.

Knowledge of Language

3. Apply knowledge of language to understand how language functions in different contexts, to make effective choices for meaning or style, and to comprehend more fully when reading or listening.
   a. Write and edit work so that it conforms to the guidelines in a style manual (e.g., *MLA Handbook*, Turabian's *Manual for Writers*) appropriate for the discipline and writing type.

Vocabulary Acquisition and Use

4. Determine or clarify the meaning of unknown and multiple-meaning words and phrases based on *grades 9–10 reading and content*, choosing flexibly from a range of strategies.

   a. Use context (e.g., the overall meaning of a sentence, paragraph, or text; a word's position or function in a sentence) as a clue to the meaning of a word or phrase.

   b. Identify and correctly use patterns of word changes that indicate different meanings or parts of speech (e.g., *analyze, analysis, analytical; advocate, advocacy*).

   c. Consult general and specialized reference materials (e.g., dictionaries, glossaries, thesauruses), both print and digital, to find the pronunciation of a word or determine or clarify its precise meaning, its part of speech, or its etymology.

   d. Verify the preliminary determination of the meaning of a word or phrase (e.g., by checking the inferred meaning in context or in a dictionary).

5. Demonstrate understanding of figurative language, word relationships, and nuances in word meanings.

   a. Interpret figures of speech (e.g., euphemism, oxymoron) in context and analyze their role in the text.

   b. Analyze nuances in the meaning of words with similar denotations.

6. Acquire and use accurately general academic and domain-specific words and phrases, sufficient for reading, writing, speaking, and listening at the college and career readiness level; demonstrate independence in gathering vocabulary knowledge when considering a word or phrase important to comprehension or expression.

10 ten

9 nine

8 eight

7 seven

6 six

5 five

4 four

3 three

2 two

1 one

ISBN 0-439-29520-3

Text copyright © MCMXCVI by Ladybird Books Ltd.
Illustrations copyright © MCMXCVI by Trevor Dunton. All rights reserved.
Published by Scholastic Inc., 555 Broadway, New York, NY 10012,
by arrangement with Ladybird Books, Ltd. SCHOLASTIC and associated logos
are trademarks and/or registered trademarks of Scholastic Inc.

12 11 10 9 8 7 6 5 4 3   10 11 12 13 14 15/0

Printed in the U.S.A.   08

First Scholastic printing, October 2001

The author/artist have asserted their moral rights.

Ten Tall Giraffes

by Brian Moses
illustrated by Trevor Dunton

SCHOLASTIC INC.

New York Toronto London Auckland Sydney
Mexico City New Delhi Hong Kong

What's the hurry?
What's the fuss?
Why are all the animals
in such a rush?

10 ten

Ten tall giraffes…

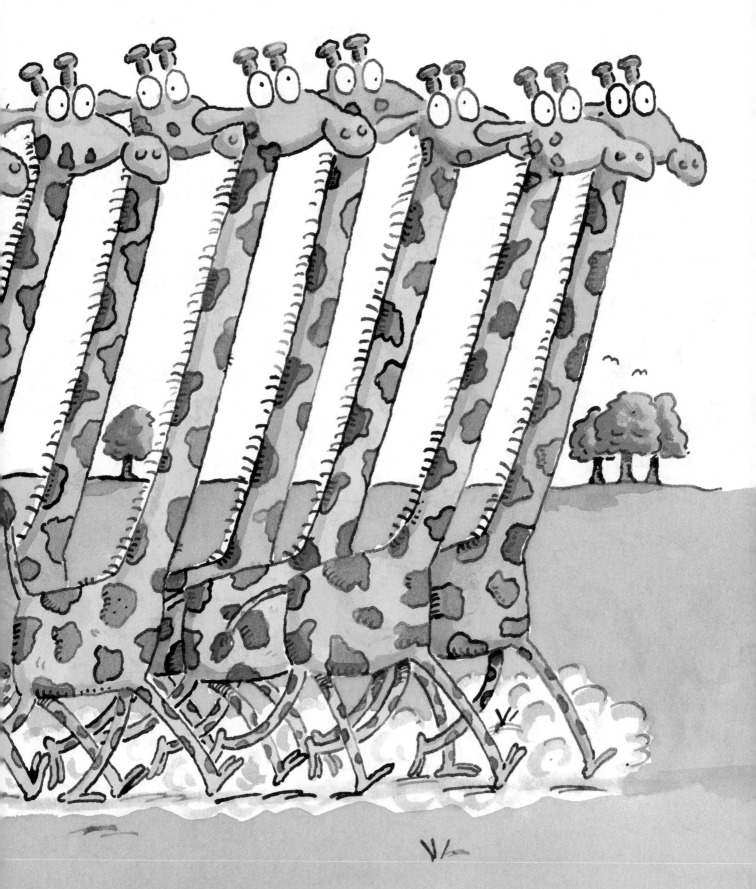

striding across the plain.

9 nine

Nine fierce tigers…

moving faster than a train.

8 eight

Eight massive whales....

racing through the sea.

7 seven

Seven silly monkeys...

swinging from tree to tree.

6 six

Six charging rhinos...

feet pounding on the ground.

5 five

Five angry bears…

making a terrible sound.

4 four

Four snapping crocodiles ...

don't get in their way!

3 three

Three excited elephants…

at the break of day.

2 two

Two jumping kangaroos …

look how high they leap!

What's the special secret
that none of them can keep?

The ten... the nine...
the eight... the seven...

the six... the five... the four...
the three... the two...

1 one

It's one enormous party...

and you're invited, too!

10 ten

9 nine

8 eight

7 seven

6 six

5 five

4 four

3 three

2 two

1 one